Arden's Housing Library

The Series Editors of Arden's Housing Library are **Andrew Arden QC** and **Caroline Hunter**. The team of expert authors is drawn from the members of Arden Chambers and other practitioners.

Arden's Housing Library provides accessible guidance to the details of housing rights and duties for those involved in the management of social housing. It breaks up the whole subject into digestible segments and approaches each topic from the perspective of its practical application. For our catalogue on other titles in the Library please call Lemos & Crane on 020 8348 8263 or email, admin@lemos.demon.co.uk.

Lydia Challen is a barrister, formerly of Arden Chambers and now employed by a London firm of solicitors.

Unauthorised and Temporary Occupation

Law and Practice in the Management of Social Housing

Lydia Challen, Barrister

Lemos & Crane

Published in Great Britain 2000 by
Lemos & Crane
20 Pond Square
Highgate
London N6 6BA
Telephone: 020 8348 8263
Fax: 020 8347 5740
Email: admin@lemos.demon.co.uk

ISBN 1-898001-50-2

A CIP catalogue record for this book is available from the British Library

Cover design by Blue Frog Ltd, London
Typeset by David Chapronière, London
Printed and bound by Redwood Books, Trowbridge

Contents

Table of Cases

Table of Statutes

Table of Statutory Instruments and Consents

Abbreviations

BC	Borough Council
CC	County Council
CCR	County Court Rules
CJPOA	Criminal Justice and Public Order Act
CLA	Criminal Law Act
CPR	Civil Procedure Rules
DC	District Council
DETR	Department of the Environment, Transport and the Regions
DoE	Department of the Environment
DPA	Defective Premises Act
DRO	displaced residential occupier
FLA	Family Law Act
HA	Housing Act
LBC	London Borough Council
LPA	Law of Property Act
LTA	Landlord and Tenant Act
PEA	Protection from Eviction Act
PIO	protected intending occupier
RSC	Rules of the Supreme Court
RSL	registered social landlord

Introduction

'Unauthorised occupation' is a term familiar to housing professionals. It is not, however, one which has a defined legal meaning, and it can cover many different situations. Literally, unauthorised occupation means occupying without permission, or, to use its legal term, trespassing. What housing managers commonly mean, however, by an unauthorised occupier is someone who is not the tenant of the property but who appears to be in occupation in the tenant's place. Such a person is not a trespasser as against the landlord until the tenancy is brought to an end.

Similarly, a person can be in unauthorised occupation of different sorts of land. The most common problem housing managers encounter is where residential property is involved, although open land is also susceptible to unauthorised occupation and specific (and probably unfamiliar) procedures are available to deal with this.

This book takes the housing manager through the legal framework so that he or she can determine whether a particular occupier is 'unauthorised' and, if so, what precise status the occupier has. It also has a separate section discussing the remedies available for trespass on open land.

There are several policy issues raised by unauthorised occupation, the most notable being how social landlords can make use of their empty property (particularly property awaiting development) and how they can ensure they house those in greatest housing need without creating security of tenure; if security is conferred on an occupier, there may be grounds for possession available. There are also issues regarding the potential liability of social landlords for the state of premises, either to those occupying them (whether with or without permission) or to neighbours. In some limited cases, the landlord can even be made liable for its failure to take action against trespassers on its property. This book discusses all these issues in detail.

When a housing manager has decided that the best course of action is to try to regain possession of the property, he or she must be aware of the necessary procedures. These begin well before a case ever comes to court. The housing manager must be aware of the rights that an occupier may have in relation to property and their implications. He or she must know what action to take to end those rights. He or she must also be able to assess the effect of various circumstances, such as the tenant's death, subletting of the premises, assignment, or the tenant ceasing to occupy the premises. These all affect the action a housing manager must take to regain possession, or even whether it is possible for the landlord to seek possession at all. Clearly, early awareness of these issues avoids unnecessary litigation and saves costs.

There are several types of procedure available for seeking possession of property and housing managers need to know which is the most appropriate for their particular case. A housing officer's main function in litigation is to collect and present evidence. This book gives a detailed account of the procedures for seeking possession and the sort of evidence a housing officer needs to support the landlord's case. There is a discussion of the defences which may be raised by an occupier so that the case against the occupier can be properly prepared and evidence rebutting such a defence can be collected. Advice is given on the presentation of evidence.

The book is in five parts. Part I looks at the policy issues facing housing officers when faced with the problem of unauthorised occupation in all its forms. Part II sets out the different sorts of occupier, their rights and how to end those rights. It includes a discussion about the rights of tenants as, commonly, a social landlord must take action against the tenant before it can tackle the problem of the unauthorised occupier. Part III discusses the common management problems housing officers encounter, with a particular emphasis on the way in which rights to occupy property can be affected by the occurrence of different events. Part IV deals with the different sorts of possession proceedings, what they are, when they are appropriate and how they should be brought. Part V looks at the problem of occupation of open land, the procedures which have been introduced to tackle this problem and the special considerations which must be taken into account.

There is also a glossary explaining the most important legal terms.

Part I

Policy Issues

1.

Policy Issues Relating to Housing Use

Empty property / Other policy issues

One of the primary functions of social landlords is to house those in greatest need who cannot otherwise afford to house themselves. The proper management of their housing stock is an essential element of carrying out this function. Not only must the stock be kept in good condition, but it must also be made available for those who need it most. Both these requirements have implications in relation to the unauthorised occupation of property.

Social landlords confront the problem that not all of their stock is in a good enough condition for use as permanent housing. Such property often lies empty and unused, perhaps because it is awaiting repair or a major development programme or simply because no consensus has been reached as to its future.

When managing the properties which are in use for permanent housing, social landlords have to be particularly aware of which of those properties are occupied by unauthorised occupants who do not have a recognised priority in terms of housing need, and of properties which are under-occupied. It is important for social landlords to gain possession of such properties so as fully to exploit their housing stock for carrying out their functions.

Empty property

While there are many good reasons why property may become empty, a social landlord wishes to keep as much of its property in use as possible. This is true particularly in the case of local authorities, which have a duty to secure that accommodation becomes available for homeless families and others in priority need. During 1997, the number of families officially recognised as homeless was 165,790; at the end of March 1998, local authorities were housing 47,080 families in temporary accommodation, such as bed and breakfast (*source*: Shelter). On 1 April 1996, a total of 103,100 properties under local authority and housing association control were empty (*source*: Empty Homes Agency). Added to these figures are the 'hidden homeless' living in unsuitable or overcrowded conditions.

Cost of empty property

It is estimated that the annual cost of keeping a single property empty is nearly £6,000. These hidden costs include loss of rent and council tax, deterioration, management costs, security and insurance. In addition, in 1996–97 the total gross cost of providing temporary accommodation for homeless households was more than £185m. Where social landlords are publicly funded, it is clearly incumbent on them to manage their property in such a way as to minimise these costs. One council was able to reduce its bed and breakfast bill from £60,000 to £1,800 by developing a good policy on using its empty property (*source*: Empty Homes Agency).

Other problems with empty property

Uninhabited property quickly falls into disrepair. The longer property is out of use, the more work and higher costs are required to make it habitable. It becomes an eyesore and possibly a danger. The landlord may be held liable for any damage which the state of the property causes (see below).

Empty property also attracts squatters. While some squatters will not cause problems, they often damage the property they are occupying. They may illegally reconnect to utilities. Their unconventional lifestyles can cause nuisance and distress to neighbours. Additionally, if squatters remain in premises for 12 years without action being taken by the landlord, they can be entitled to claim ownership of the property. In this way valuable housing stock can be lost.

Empty properties can become the focus of criminal activity. The most common is vandalism, but they can be used for crimes such as drug dealing. Clearly this has an adverse effect on the lives of those living nearby. Vandalism puts neighbouring properties more at risk of being directly vandalised and of damage being caused by the condition of the empty property itself. It is not uncommon for vandals to start fires in empty properties which can spread to those around.

The result is that the area may become stigmatised. If the area appears insecure to live in, transfer requests increase which in turn leads to more empty properties, which can mean more vandalism and an increase in criminal activity. This cycle can result in the area becoming 'hard to let'. This increases void times of properties in the area between lettings. To overcome these problems the landlord may have to offer properties in excess of the housing need of the applicant or offer enhanced repairs packages, thus increasing expenditure.

Landlords need to be aware that they can be liable to any visitor to the property who is injured as a result of the state of the property, and to trespassers in certain circumstances. They can even be liable for nuisance or damage caused to neighbours by trespassers on the property. All these issues are dealt with further in Chapter 4.

Government advice

The Government issues circulars to advise local authorities in carrying out their functions. Although not legally binding, the authority must consider such advice before taking any action. The Department of the Environment (DoE—now the Department of the Environment, Transport and the Regions) issued Circular 12/85, 'Local Authority Empty Dwellings', in 1985. In this circular, local authorities are asked to take all possible steps *as a matter of priority* to reduce the number of empty properties. Various methods of doing this are suggested, in particular:

- better management of reletting procedures, which involves a shorter turnaround time for empty properties and expediting repair and redecoration work necessary before reletting;
- better management of improvement programmes, which involves trying to minimise the need to decant tenants when improvement works are undertaken;
- greater use of short-life schemes and temporary lettings (see Chap. 3); and
- sales to the private sector.

Local authorities are advised to work together with housing associations and other social landlords in tackling the problem of empty properties.

Other policy issues

Housing those in greatest need

Many unauthorised occupiers, whether they are squatters or holding over after the end of a tenancy of property owned by social landlords, are not people considered to be in the greatest housing need. They may be perfectly willing to pay rent if granted a tenancy of the property. They may be very reliable and conscientious. It is not uncommon for such occupiers to have been exploited by the tenant subletting the property to them without permission (sometimes claiming housing benefit at the same time). Preference must, however, be shown to those in greatest housing need.

Local authorities have to be particularly aware of their new duties in terms of allocation of housing under the

Housing Act (HA) 1996. Every time a local authority grants a secure tenancy, it makes an 'allocation' which, by section 167(8) of HA 1996, must be in accordance with its allocations policy. This means that, where secure tenancies are inadvertently granted to unauthorised occupiers (e.g. by the mistaken acceptance of rent), the local authority could be in breach of its allocations policy. It is clearly not desirable for local authorities to act contrary to statutory requirements in this way.

Housing officers must therefore act quickly to seek possession of such property. In many cases, delay works to the disadvantage of occupiers who may be liable to pay damages to the landlord for the period during which they unlawfully occupied the premises. Housing benefit may not be available and, even if it is, it is unlikely that the occupiers will have made a claim. Occupiers may then be subject to a money judgment which they will not have anticipated and which can run to four figures or more.

Under-occupation

When properties are occupied by unauthorised occupiers, there is no question of matching a property to the needs of the occupier. Frequently this results in the under-occupation of property. This commonly occurs when the unauthorised occupation results from the death of the previous tenant without any person being qualified to succeed to the tenancy (see generally Chap. 8). Given the (usually) higher ratio between demand and supply for larger property, it is clearly important for social landlords to repossess such properties to optimise their use.

2.

Giving Use with Security

The danger of creating security / Possession where security has been granted

As discussed in Chapter 1, there are significant disadvantages to social landlords in keeping property empty. By the very nature of their housing management functions, however, it is inevitable that social landlords will have responsibility for properties which are not currently suitable for letting on a permanent basis. These are properties that are awaiting major repairs or that are part of a larger redevelopment proposal. It may even be that the properties have been compulsorily purchased pending demolition to make way for a development such as a road. In all these cases, the pressure on housing stock is such that social landlords will want to use the property rather than see it standing empty.

The danger of creating security

The social landlord must have possession of the properties when proposed works are ready to go ahead. This may be a question of waiting for tenants who have security of tenure to leave or for successful possession proceedings to be brought against them. It is also often a case of waiting for funding for the programme of works or development to become available. Once funding is in place, it may only be available for a relatively short period, such as one financial year. Funding is often from an external source and is simply allocated elsewhere if the project is not ready to proceed. In an age when funding is not easy to come by, social landlords cannot afford to let chances for redevelopment slip by simply as a result of inefficient management.

The main danger of granting secure tenancies or secure licences of property awaiting development is that it restricts the landlord's flexibility. It is not possible to predict when possession can be regained or to know that possession can be obtained quickly when required. Landlords must demonstrate grounds for possession and may need to provide occupiers with suitable alternative accommodation. Depending on the ground on which possession is sought, the court may have a discretion whether to order possession. It can also suspend the operation of any possession order either when the order is made or on application by the tenant when the warrant for possession is issued.

This danger of losing flexibility is not so acute for housing associations and other non-local authority social landlords, which can grant assured shorthold tenancies (although RSLs must have regard to Housing Corporation guidance, discussed below). These have a very quick and simple procedure for obtaining possession; once the correct notice has been served under section 21 of HA 1996, the court must order possession. The only constraint is that no order for possession will be made to take effect less than six months from the date of the grant of the original tenancy.

Other dangers

The grant of a tenancy can bring with it other duties which are imposed on the landlord by statute, principally repairing obligations. These duties are imposed whether or not the tenant has any security of tenure. They may also be imposed even where both parties are under the impression that the landlord is only granting a licence (see pp. 49–50).

Implied into every tenancy granted after 24 October 1961 for less than seven years is an obligation on the landlord to keep the structure and exterior of the property in repair, together with any installations for the supply of water, gas and electricity, for sanitation and for space and water heating (Landlord and Tenant Act (LTA) 1985, s. 11: see further A. Kilpatrick, *Dealing with Disrepair* (Arden's Housing Library, 1996), ch. 2). Clearly where premises are awaiting major redevelopment, a social landlord will not want to spend large amounts of money to comply with a repairing covenant.

The standard of repair required from any landlord depends on the property's prospective life. Some element of sensitivity to the property's future is therefore built into the duty on the landlord; accordingly, where the premises have been scheduled for demolition or complete rebuilding, a property can be in serious disrepair, without the landlord having to carry out extensive repair works. Where plans are more nebulous, however, or the property is not coming to the end of its useful life, a social landlord is required to fulfil its repairing obligations to a normal standard of repair.

Case reports

In 1973, Newham LBC let to Mr Patel a house which suffered badly from damp and other defects. The rent for the property was very low to reflect its poor condition. In 1977, the public health inspector confirmed that the property was unfit for human habitation and identified an extensive list of works required. The local authority took the view that temporary repairs would not be effective and that complete redevelopment would be required, and sought to rehouse Mr Patel. He refused to move and so the local authority commenced possession proceedings. Mr Patel counterclaimed for damages for the disrepair. The Court of Appeal held that the limited prospective life of the house affected the standard of repair required under the predecessor of section 11 of LTA 1985. The authority was not bound to carry out repairs which would be wholly useless. Thus there was no breach of the local authority's repairing obligations. In addition, the very low rent paid by Mr Patel would have affected any award of damages to him. *Newham LBC v Patel* (1978)

Ms McLean, a secure tenant of Liverpool City Council, sued the authority for breach of section 11 of LTA 1985, complaining of severe dampness. At the trial she produced a report from her surveyor which set out the defects. It also stated that the house was lacking a bathroom and inside toilet and that, even if all the repairs were carried out, the house still needed complete modernisation if its life was to be extended. The authority agreed the report and called no evidence of its own. The judge accepted that there were problems of rising damp. He went on to decide, however, that having regard to the age, character and prospective life of the house, its location and the fact that there was a nominal rent, there was no breach of section 11. The Court of Appeal overturned his decision and ordered a new trial. There was no evidence that the rent was nominal, nor that repairs would be wholly useless, nor as to the prospective life of the house. There was, therefore, no basis for the judge's decision. *McLean v Liverpool City Council* (1987)

Possession where security has been granted

There may be circumstances where a social landlord has either inadvertently granted a secure or assured tenancy of property which is needed for redevelopment or there are existing secure or assured tenants living in the property whom the landlord needs to remove in order to carry out its plans. There are grounds for possession which may be available in this situation.

Grounds for possession of secure tenancies

Grounds 10 and 10A of Schedule 2 to HA 1985 are often available to a local authority when it intends to redevelop property. Possession is only ordered where suitable alternative accommodation is available for the tenant.

Ground 10 is satisfied where the landlord intends within a reasonable time of obtaining possession of the dwelling house to:

- demolish or reconstruct the building or part of the building comprising the dwelling house; or
- carry out work on the building or on land let together with the building;

and cannot reasonably do so without obtaining possession. The landlord must give evidence that possession is required and that the redevelopment will be carried out within a reasonable time of obtaining possession.

Ground 10A is satisfied where (a) the whole or part of the dwelling house is in an area subject to a redevelopment scheme approved by the Secretary of State (or, in the case of secure tenancies granted by registered housing associations before 1 January 1989, the Housing Corporation) and (b) the landlord intends within a reasonable time of obtaining possession to dispose of the whole or part of the dwelling house in accordance with the scheme. This ground therefore applies when the development is to be carried out by someone other than the landlord.

Ground for possession of assured tenancies

Ground 6 of Schedule 2 to HA 1988 is similar to ground 10 of HA 1985. It is, however, a mandatory ground and there is no requirement for the landlord to provide suitable alternative accommodation. The ground applies when the landlord or, in the case of a registered social landlord (RSL) or a charitable housing trust, its superior landlord intends to demolish, reconstruct or carry out substantial works to the whole or part of the dwelling house. The intended work must be such that it cannot reasonably be carried out for one of the following reasons:

- the tenant is not willing to agree to a variation of the terms of the tenancy which would allow the landlord the access and other facilities required to carry out the work; or
- the nature of the work is such that no such variation is possible; or
- the tenant is not willing to accept an assured tenancy of only a part of the dwelling house, thus giving the landlord possession of so much of the rest of the house as would be reasonable to enable the work to be carried out, or to allow such access or other facilities over the part which the tenant retains to permit the work to be carried out; or
- the nature of the work is such that such a tenancy is not practicable.

The ground is not available to a landlord which acquired its interest in the property for money or money's worth after the tenancy had been granted.

As there is no requirement to provide suitable alternative accommodation, a claim for possession on this ground is likely to be strongly contested, particularly over whether the work cannot reasonably be carried out without the tenant giving up possession. A social landlord must therefore be prepared with expert evidence on this issue.

Key points

- Creating tenancies which have security of tenure or secure licences can result in a loss of flexibility over development of the premises.
- Creating tenancies of any kind can result in the landlord being subject to repairing obligations.
- Where security of tenure has been granted, social landlords may be able to seek possession on grounds 10 and 10A of Schedule 2 to HA 1985 (where suitable alternative accommodation must be provided for the tenant) or on ground 6 of Schedule 2 to HA 1988 (which is mandatory).

3.

Giving Use without Security

Use of empty property without security

As Chapter 2 illustrates, it is clearly preferable to use empty property without creating security. This chapter looks at the various circumstances in which empty property can be put back into residential use without creating security.

The mere fact that an arrangement does not give security is no guarantee that it will be possible to recover possession of the premises immediately it is required. The volume of litigation involving these kinds of arrangements bears witness to that. It does, however, provide much more certainty that possession will be recovered than if security is created. Social landlords therefore have to weigh the advantages of using empty property to perform their function of housing those most in need against the consequences of their possible inability to have possession of the premises exactly when it is required.

Social landlords ought also to be aware that the grant of a tenancy, whether or not it has security, carries with it certain rights. Most importantly, repairing obligations are implied on the part of the landlord (see p. 14 above). In those circumstances (and particularly in the case of local authority landlords), it is possible to licence the properties to organisations such as co-operative housing associations which will themselves carry out necessary patch repairs, making the premises habitable.

Use of empty property without security

The various ways of using empty property without creating security include:

- the use of property acquired for development
- the use of property to discharge functions under Part VII of HA 1996
- other temporary uses
- tolerating the presence of trespassers
- setting up 'shortlife' arrangements between local authorities and housing associations.

The advantages and disadvantages of these uses are explored below. Most of them principally relate to the use of property by local authorities. Subject to the advice produced by the Housing Corporation, RSLs can avoid most of the problems by creating assured shorthold tenancies whereby possession can be recovered six months after the tenancy is granted.

Housing Corporation advice

The Housing Corporation has published a policy which must be observed by RSLs on the grant of assured shorthold tenancies (Circular R3-36/96). In general, RSLs are expected to grant assured tenancies. Assured shorthold tenancies may only be used in defined circumstances, which include the use of housing which is time limited and providing accommodation for homeless persons.

Use of development land

Local authorities can exploit the exceptions to security set out in Schedule 1 to HA 1985 to grant tenancies or licences which are not secure. Some of these exceptions are once and for all exclusions from security. In relation to others, the exclusion will apply only for so long as certain conditions apply. The exception in relation to development land falls into the second category.

A tenancy or licence is not secure if the dwelling house is on land acquired for development and is used by the landlord, pending development of the land, as temporary housing accommodation (Sched. 1, para. 3). In this context, development means 'the carrying out of any building, engineering, mining or other operations in, on, and over or under land, or the making of any material change in the use of buildings or other land' (Town and Country Planning Act 1990, s. 55(1)). It does not include works which affect only the interior of the premises. The conversion of a single dwelling house to several flats would be a change of use and therefore development.

It is not essential that the land has been acquired or that the development is to be carried out by the landlord letting the premises. This means that a local authority could grant non-secure tenancies or licences of land which has been compulsorily purchased by a government department for road widening purposes even though the local authority would have no involvement in the development (*Hyde Housing Association v Harrison* (1990)).

As development is a long-term process, it does not matter that it may take a long time for any action to be taken in relation to the development as long as the development can truly be said to be 'pending'. The exception has been held to apply where premises were let on fixed-term ten-year leases. Given the long-term nature of development, this could still be seen as use as temporary housing accommodation. Nor does it matter if, owing to a change in circumstances, the proposed development changes to something different from the development for which the property was originally acquired (*Attley v Cherwell DC* (1989)).

It is different, however, if development plans are shelved without there being any further plans for the property's future. In this case, development cannot properly be said to be 'pending', the exception will no longer apply and any tenancy or licence of the premises will become secure (unless there are other reasons excepting it from security).

Case report

Lambeth LBC compulsorily purchased an area of 29 houses in 1971 and, in 1978, made a rehabilitation order in respect of some of those properties. In 1981 the local authority licensed the houses to a housing association which in turn sub-licensed the houses to the Lillieshall Road Housing Co-operative. The Brennans were original members of the co-operative and moved into the houses in 1981. In 1990, the co-operative served them with a notice to quit on the basis that they were not secure tenants by reason of paragraph 3 of Schedule 1 to HA 1985. At the trial, the authority gave evidence showing that it was uncertain whether the property would be redeveloped and that possible proposals for redevelopment had not been accepted by the (then) DoE. The Court of Appeal held that in the light of that evidence it was impossible to say that development was pending. The exception to security therefore did not apply and the Brennans were secure tenants. *Lillieshall Road Housing Co-operative v Brennan* (1991)

Use of property to house the homeless

The exception from security of property used to house the homeless is found in paragraph 4 of Schedule 1 to HA 1985. Local authorities have duties to house the homeless under Part VII of HA 1996. This may involve the provision of accommodation at several stages. Where a local authority grants a right to occupy property as a result of those duties, the tenancy or licence cannot be secure unless the local authority notifies the tenant or licensee that it *is* to be secure. Any such notification amounts to an allocation under Part VI of HA 1996 and so must be in accordance with the local authority's allocations policy.

This means that local authorities can under the HA 1996 provisions provide the following accommodation without it being secure:

- interim accommodation pending enquiries for those whom the local authority has reason to believe may be homeless, eligible for assistance and in priority need (s. 188);
- interim accommodation for those whom the local authority is satisfied are homeless, eligible for assistance, in priority need but homeless intentionally (s. 190);
- interim accommodation pending a decision to refer an applicant to another local authority (s. 200);
- interim accommodation as above pending an appeal to the county court (s. 204);
- accommodation in discharge of the full housing duty to those who are unintentionally homeless, eligible for assistance and in priority need. This accommodation can be provided for a maximum of two years unless it is hostel accommodation or leased from a private sector landlord (see further below).

Local authorities can make arrangements with housing associations and other RSLs for them to provide accommodation in discharge of duties to the homeless. If an RSL so grants a right to occupy accommodation there are limitations to the security that can be conferred. If the accommodation is provided pursuant to an interim duty (under s. 188, 190, 200 or 204), the tenancy is not an assured (or assured shorthold) tenancy until 12 months from the date of (a) notification of the local authority's decision, (b) any reviewed decision, or (c) the result of any appeal, unless the landlord notifies the occupant otherwise. An RSL can only serve a notice making the tenancy an assured *shorthold* tenancy. Where the provision of accommodation is pursuant to a full housing duty, an RSL may only grant an assured shorthold tenancy unless the accommodation is allocated to the occupant in accordance with the provisions of Part VI of HA 1996.

Temporary accommodation from private landlords

As well as RSLs themselves providing accommodation as outlined above, it is also possible for any private landlord to lease property to a local authority with vacant possession for use as temporary housing accommodation. Where the following conditions are satisfied, any tenancies or licences of that property granted by the local authority will not be secure:

- the terms of the lease between the private landlord and the local authority enable the landlord to regain vacant possession on the expiry of a specified period or when required by the landlord;
- the private landlord is not capable of granting secure tenancies; and
- the local authority has no interest in the property except under the lease in question or as a mortgagee (i.e. the lender under a mortgage).

Granting such leases to local authorities can be a useful way for RSLs who cannot grant secure tenancies to put their empty properties to use without creating security. The advantage of this arrangement over simply granting assured shorthold tenancies of the property is that there is no requirement that the tenancy should be a minimum of six months.

Other temporary uses

Local authorities can grant tenancies to students and to persons moving into the area for employment purposes without granting security. In both cases the local authority must inform the prospective tenant of the circumstances in which the exception applies and that in its opinion the proposed tenancy will fall within the exception. Such tenancies are not secure unless the local authority informs the tenant that the tenancy is to be secure. In general, the position may be the same if the authority grants a licence rather than a tenancy (see further pp. 61–62 below).

Students

The exception for student accommodation is found in paragraph 10 of Schedule 1. A tenancy is not secure if it is granted to enable the tenant to attend a designated course at an educational establishment. In general terms, a course is designated if it is:

- one which attracts a mandatory award; or
- a post-graduate course; or
- any other full-time course provided by an establishment of further education maintained or assisted out of public funds.

The notice which the landlord is required to give (see above) must also specify the educational establishment which the person concerned proposes to attend.

Persons taking up employment

This exception is found in paragraph 5 of Schedule 1. The conditions necessary for it to apply are that:

- the person to whom the tenancy was granted was not, immediately before the grant, resident in the district in which the dwelling house is situated;
- before the grant of the tenancy, he or she obtained employment, or an offer of employment, in the district or its surrounding area; and
- the tenancy was granted to meet his or her need for temporary accommodation in the district or its surrounding area in order to work there, and to enable him or her to find permanent accommodation there.

Allowing the property to be squatted

Temporary interests granted as an expedient to those who enter property as trespassers will not have security (see also Chap. 6). There may be a temptation therefore simply to wait until empty property becomes squatted and then to regularise such an arrangement afterwards. There are many disadvantages to such an approach:

- the landlord has no control over who enters into occupation of the premises;

- the premises may not be used to house those who are in greatest need;
- there is a risk that the premises will be vandalised, both while lying empty and while occupied by trespassers;
- in turn this can have a stigmatising effect on the area and the surrounding properties can become hard to let;
- there is a risk that the landlord will fail to regularise the occupants' position and that the occupants will ultimately be able to establish 'adverse possession' (see Chap. 15). This results in the landlord losing ownership of the premises altogether.

Shortlife arrangements

A local authority can bring property into residential use while avoiding creating security by virtue of what are often called 'shortlife schemes'. These involve letting the property to a housing association on a tenancy or a licence. The housing association then uses the property for temporary accommodation. When the local authority requires the property for redevelopment, either the housing association provides vacant possession or the authority terminates the association's tenancy or licence. The rights of occupation granted by the housing association are not binding on the local authority and determining the housing association's interest also operates to determine any interest of the remaining occupiers. The local authority can then bring proceedings for possession against the housing association and all the residents of the property.

Setting up shortlife arrangements

The detail of the setting-up of these arrangements is beyond the scope of this book. There are, however, some basic principles which should be borne in mind.

First, a local authority would be well advised to grant only licences to housing associations for the following reasons:

1. While a housing association does not have security of tenure under HA 1985 because it is not an individual, it

may be protected by the Landlord and Tenant Act (LTA) 1954. This gives tenants who occupy premises for business purposes a right to an automatic continuation of their existing tenancy and the ability in certain circumstances to apply for a new tenancy. This protection does not apply to licences or tenancies at will. A tenancy at will is a tenancy the terms of which allow either party to determine the tenancy at any time. True tenancies at will are rare.

2. The local authority may be required to obtain the Secretary of State's permission before granting a lease to an RSL (HA 1985, s. 32; General Consents for the Disposal of Houses and Land 1999).

Where a local authority is leasing property which will be subject to redevelopment, it is probable that it will require unrestricted access to assess the premises' condition, carry out surveys, draw up redevelopment plans etc. In this case, the local authority can grant a licence to the housing association as it will not part with exclusive possession of the premises (see also Chap. 5).

The second principle to bear in mind is that the arrangement with the housing association must not simply amount to an agreement whereby the association acts as the local authority's agent. Here, the tenancies granted by the housing association are binding on the local authority. It is usual therefore for the housing association to be given a certain amount of autonomy over the way that it selects its tenants or licensees. It is also common for there to be a term in the licence agreement that the housing association is not to grant tenancies (although see pp. 49–50 below).

Operation of the arrangement

Housing associations should usually seek only to grant licences of shortlife property where they are licensees themselves and do not have the capacity to grant tenancies. They can only do this, however, where there is a genuine reason for them not to grant exclusive possession of the premises (e.g. because they need to retain the right to move occupants between rooms, or because they provide services which require access to the premises). Even where a housing association informs the prospective occupier of its lack of capacity, if the agreement bears all the hallmarks of a tenancy, as between the housing association and the occupant, a tenancy is created (*Bruton v London and Quadrant Housing Association* (1999)).

If the housing association grants tenancies, they are generally assured tenancies. This is so (between the tenant and the housing association) whether or not the housing association has permission to do so. In the case of a co-operative housing association, however, any tenancies it grants will be outside security altogether. Local authorities may therefore be keen to operate such shortlife agreements with co-operative housing associations to enable vacant possession of the premises to be obtained easily when it is needed.

Co-operative housing associations

A co-operative housing association is a fully mutual housing association which is a society registered under the Industrial and Provident Societies Act 1965. A fully mutual housing association is a housing association whose rules:

- restrict membership to persons who are tenants or prospective tenants of the association, and
- preclude the granting or assignment of tenancies to persons other than members.

Termination by housing association of rights of occupation

Where the housing association has granted tenancies, the normal termination rules apply, most likely in relation to assured or assured shorthold tenancies. Ground 6 of Schedule 2 to HA 1988 (see above) often applies in shortlife arrangements where the local authority head landlord wishes to redevelop the property. Where licences have been granted, the housing association simply has to give the appropriate period of notice (see also Chap. 7).

Termination of the shortlife arrangement

If the local authority requires the premises for redevelopment, it must terminate the housing association's interest. All the interests created by the housing association will then come to an end. If the housing association has a licence, this can be revoked by notice. A tenancy at will can be brought to an end by a demand for possession.

The local authority is not in general bound by the tenancies granted by the housing association. An exception to this rule operates if the association has a tenancy which it surrenders (for which see Chap. 8). The effect of a surrender is that any sub-tenants of the housing association, whether lawful or unlawful, become the local authority's tenants. As they are individuals there is nothing to prevent them from being secure tenants. In general, therefore, a local authority must not accept a surrender from a housing association under a shortlife arrangement unless the housing association has itself acquired vacant possession of the premises.

There is another advantage of the local authority only granting a licence to the housing association. If the housing association purports to grant tenancies to the occupiers, while as against the housing association the occupiers have the rights of assured tenants, the local authority is not bound by such tenancies. This is the case even if the housing association relinquishes its rights under the licence.

Once the housing association's interest is brought to an end, proceedings for possession of the premises can be brought. It will probably be necessary to join all the residents of the property as parties to the proceedings.

Case report

Camden LBC made an arrangement with Shortlife Community Housing ('SCH') that it should manage certain buildings on Gray's Inn Road. The buildings were awaiting redevelopment but still contained some secure tenants. The vacant parts of the buildings were licensed to SCH which then gave licences to its own members. It was not permitted to grant tenancies under its licence agreement. When all the secure tenants had left, Camden wanted possession for redevelopment and so served notice to quit in accordance with the licence agreement. SCH defended the proceedings on the basis that it was a protected tenant under the LTA 1954 and the occupiers claimed that they had tenancies of the flats they occupied.

It was held that Camden never intended to part with exclusive possession of the premises having regard to all the circumstances—the purpose of the arrangements, the short-term nature of the accommodation, the fluidity of the financial arrangements, the nominal weekly licence fee which bore no relation to the size of the property, the fact that it was SCH rather than the occupiers who were treated as being in paramount occupancy and Camden's need to retain rights of access in view of the perceived imminence of demolition and reconstruction. Further, SCH had only granted licences to its occupants but, even if it had granted tenancies, those tenancies could not have bound Camden as SCH did not have the capacity to grant them. The arrangement was not protected by the LTA 1954 for two reasons: first, SCH only had a licence, and secondly, the services supplied by SCH to its occupants were not sufficient to say that SCH was in occupation of the flats for the purposes of its business. *Camden LBC v Shortlife Community Housing* (1992)

Key points

Local authorities can give use of property without creating security by:

- using property which has been acquired for development as temporary housing accommodation;
- using property to perform their functions under Part VII of HA 1996;
- letting property to students to enable them to attend a designated course;

- letting property to persons taking up employment in the area;
- entering into shortlife arrangements with a housing association or housing co-operative;
- tolerating the presence of squatters.

Other social landlords can use properties in the short term by:

- tolerating the presence of squatters;
- granting a lease to a local authority for use as temporary accommodation;
- granting licences of the premises;
- granting assured shorthold tenancies.

4.

Liability for Premises

Who is an occupier? / Liability to those on the premises / Liability to those not on the premises

Whether social landlords use their empty properties or not, they must be aware of their potential liability for the state of their premises. The ownership or occupation of premises carries with it certain duties to make sure that they are not a danger to those who may enter them or to those who are not on the premises but who may be affected by their defects. Social landlords will be familiar with the duties they have to their tenants (see further A. Kilpatrick, *Repairs and Maintenance* (Arden's Housing Library, 1996)). However, there are also duties in respect of their unoccupied properties, for example empty properties awaiting demolition or major works programmes. The extent of these duties depends on the nature of a social landlord's control over the premises and the type of person affected by any defect (e.g. whether they are trespassers or licensees of the social landlord).

Who is an occupier?

Generally a person is an occupier of premises if he or she has a sufficient degree of physical control over the premises to be able to ensure they are safe. An occupier need not actually have any legal interest in the premises as long as he or she has a right to possession of the premises and to permit others to come onto the premises. There can be more than one occupier of premises; thus, a builder carrying on work on the premises may be an occupier as well as the owner. A social landlord, being a body corporate, must occupy premises through its employees.

When a landlord lets premises to a tenant, it gives to the tenant 'exclusive possession' of them. The landlord therefore parts with control, and does so even though it may be liable to repair the premises. In this situation, the landlord is not an occupier, although it has other liabilities because of its position as a landlord (see below). In some cases where the landlord grants a licence, it may also part with control sufficiently so as not to be considered an occupier, although this depends on the facts of each case. A landlord, however, remains the occupier of any parts of the premises which it retains (e.g. the common parts).

Of particular relevance to local authorities is the fact that requisitioning authorities and authorities acquiring property by compulsory purchase are likely to be treated as occupiers of the premises even where the premises are being wholly used by the licensees of the authority. The authority is deemed to be an occupier from the moment the previous occupants leave rather than from the date when the authority actually enters the property.

Where a social landlord leaves premises empty and unlet, whether until a major works programme begins or merely because the previous tenant has left and the premises have not been relet, it is an occupier of those premises.

Case report

Chelsea BC requisitioned a property to be used to accommodate the homeless. Mr Greene applied to the authority for accommodation for himself and his family and was offered the property on a licence under Chelsea's emergency powers. In May 1951, Mrs Greene noticed a bulge in the kitchen ceiling and reported it to Chelsea, whose workmen inspected the ceiling but did nothing to repair it. In December 1951, the ceiling collapsed on top of Mrs Greene who brought an action for personal injury against Chelsea. By the time the action was heard, Mr Greene had died. The Court of Appeal held that Chelsea, as a requisitioning authority, remained in possession of the requisitioned premises despite granting a licence to Mr Greene and his family and that Chelsea therefore owed a duty to all the family to make sure that the property was reasonably safe for their occupation. Chelsea had failed to do so and was therefore liable for Mrs Greene's injuries. *Greene v Chelsea BC* (1954)

Liability to those on the premises

A social landlord may be liable for injuries sustained by or damage to the property of those who come onto its premises. The extent of this liability depends on whether the social landlord has parted with possession or whether it is in fact an occupier of the premises.

Where social landlord parts with possession

A landlord may part with possession by granting exclusive possession of the premises to someone else, either on a tenancy or on a licence. Where a social landlord grants a tenancy, it is no longer the occupier of premises. It has obligations to its tenant, however, as a result of its repairing covenants and by virtue of the Defective Premises Act 1972.

A landlord's liability to his tenant to repair under his repairing covenants is beyond the scope of this book (but see further A. Kilpatrick, *Repairs and Maintenance* (Arden's Housing Library, 1996)).

Under the general law, a landlord is liable to its tenant for any injury suffered because of defects in the property which were created by the landlord's own negligence, whether before or after the lease was entered into (*Rimmer v Liverpool City*

Council (1985); *Targett v Torfaen BC* (1992)). In addition, where the landlord has granted a licence of the premises, it may also be liable for injury suffered owing to defects which are not of its own making where it knows or ought reasonably to have known the state of the premises (*Graham v NI Housing Executive* (1986); *Greene v Chelsea BC*—see 'Case report' above).

Defective Premises Act 1972

The Defective Premises Act (DPA) 1972 imposes two main duties on a social landlord. The first arises when the landlord does works to premises (s. 3), and the second when it fails to do works (s. 4). In both cases, a landlord can be liable not only to any tenant or licensee, but to any other person who might reasonably be expected to be affected by the defects. This includes those living with the tenant or licensee, their visitors and people outside the premises such as neighbours or users of the highway.

Where a social landlord does works to premises (for instance of construction, maintenance or repairs), it is vital that the works are done properly. If:

1. the works are done inadequately,
2. the works therefore cause defects in the premises, and
3. those defects go on to cause injury to any person as detailed above,

the landlord is liable for that injury. By section 3 of DPA 1972, this liability persists even though the premises may have been let on a tenancy. This means that a landlord continues to be liable for defects caused by works whenever they were carried out.

Section 4 of DPA 1972 applies to premises let on both leases and licences. Where:

- there is an agreement under which the landlord or licensor has either an *obligation* to repair or maintain the premises or a *right* to enter onto the premises to carry out works of maintenance or repair, and
- the landlord is in a position to exercise that right, and

- the landlord fails to repair the premises in accordance with its obligations or it fails to exercise its right of entry, and
- this failure leads to defects in the premises, and
- as a result of those defects, any person who might reasonably be expected to be affected by them suffers injury or damage to his or her property,

then the landlord is liable for that injury or damage.

Where social landlord is an occupier

A social landlord is the occupier of any of its properties over which it has direct control. It is usually considered to be the occupier of its empty properties as it has control over them and ought to be able to ensure their safety. Because of this ability to control the premises, the law imposes duties on occupiers over the state of their premises. The duty a social landlord owes to persons who have permission to be on the premises ('visitors', as governed by the Occupiers' Liability Act 1957) is different from the duty it owes to trespassers (under the Occupiers' Liability Act 1984).

Liability to visitors

Visitors are those who have permission to be on the premises. They include workmen and housing officers. Permission to be on the premises need not be express, and can be implied from the circumstances. For instance, a person entering the premises to have dealings with the occupier (e.g. a double glazing salesperson or a beggar) is a visitor as long as he or she remains on that part of the premises which provides the usual access to the premises (e.g. the front path) unless there is a sign displayed forbidding entry. Children have been held to be visitors despite not having permission to be on the premises where the occupier puts something which he or she ought to know is particularly enticing to children near the boundary of the premises. In a sense the occupier is deemed to have invited them onto the premises.

Permission may be limited to a specific part of the premises or to a specific period of time. If the visitor strays into other parts of the premises or overstays his or her welcome, he or she becomes a trespasser.

Those who have a legal right to enter the premises are classed as visitors. For example, a police officer with a search warrant or a gas meter reader are visitors whether or not the occupier consents to their presence.

A social landlord owes its visitors a duty to take such care as is reasonable in the circumstances to see that the visitor is reasonably safe in using the premises for the purposes for which he or she is invited or permitted to be there. This also extends to the property of others which is on the premises. This duty is known as the 'common duty of care' (Occupiers' Liability Act 1957). What care is reasonable in the circumstances depends on many factors, including:

- how obvious the danger is,
- the visitor's age
- the purpose of his or her visit
- the occupier's state of knowledge
- any warnings put up by the occupier, and
- the expense of removing the danger.

Putting up a warning does not allow the occupier to escape liability unless in all the circumstances it is enough to allow the visitor to be reasonably safe.

Children

A social landlord must be prepared for children to be less careful than adults. Also there are things which, whilst not a danger to adults, are a danger to children, such as railings which are too far apart to prevent a small child from falling through them. A social landlord must ensure that children cannot gain access to such dangers.

Visitors in the course of business

Where a visitor is on the premises because of his or her job, an occupier is entitled to expect that the visitor will guard against any risks which are normally an aspect of his or her activity. So, for instance, a window cleaner could not recover for an injury sustained when ornamental trelliswork broke away while he was cleaning the windows and he lost his balance and fell (*Caddis v Gettrup* (1967)). This rule would not prevent the occupier from being liable if the window cleaner had been injured when the ceiling fell in on top of him because of defective plasterwork.

If a fire starts in an empty property as the result of the occupier's negligence (e.g. if he or she keeps highly flammable materials on the property in such a way that they are likely to ignite), the occupier could be liable to a fireman who is foreseeably injured while trying to put out the fire.

Defences to liability

It is a defence to liability for an occupier to show that he or she did all that he or she reasonably could in the circumstances to protect the visitor from harm. An occupier is not liable for injury to the visitor which is sustained as a result of risks willingly run by the visitor. The occupier may also argue that the visitor was careless and so must bear at least part of the blame for the accident.

Exclusion of liability

A social landlord's liability under the common duty of care can, in general, be excluded either by agreement or by putting up a notice on the premises informing visitors that they enter at their own risk. However, a local authority cannot exclude liability for its own negligence which results in a visitor's death or personal injury; nor can it unreasonably exclude its liability for other loss or damage (Unfair Contract Terms Act 1977, ss. 2 and 14).

Case report

A boat was abandoned on grass beside a block of flats owned by Sutton LBC and remained there for two years. The boat appeared sound, but was rotten. The council was aware of it but, because of a bureaucratic muddle, failed to move it. The 14-year-old plaintiff and his friend decided to repair the boat to sail it. They worked on it for six weeks, using a car jack to prop it up. The plaintiff was working under the boat when it moved, landing on his back and crushing him. He was rendered paraplegic and confined to a wheelchair. He sued the council for personal injury. The Court of Appeal held that the council was negligent for failing to remove the boat. It was foreseeable that children might play around the boat and injure themselves because of its rotten condition. It was not, however, reasonably foreseeable that an accident would occur because of a child's decision to prop up the boat and work underneath it. The council was therefore not liable for the plaintiff's injuries. *Jolley v Sutton LBC* (1998)

Liability to trespassers

The Occupiers' Liability Act 1984 sets out the duty which an occupier owes to those who trespass on his or her premises. An occupier has a duty to a trespasser where

- he or she knows or ought to know of the existence of a danger on the premises;
- he or she knows or has reasonable grounds to believe that the trespasser is either in or may come into the vicinity of the danger; and
- the risk is one against which in all the circumstances of the case he or she may reasonably be expected to offer the trespasser some protection.

The duty is to take such care as is reasonable in the circumstances to see that the trespasser does not suffer injury on the premises as a result of the danger.

As the duty depends on all the circumstances, the occupier must consider two aspects in particular:

- the seriousness of the danger—the more serious the danger, the more effective the steps that must be taken to keep the trespasser away;

- the type of trespasser likely to come—an occupier must take much greater care for the safety of child trespassers than for adults.

Discharge of the duty

The duty is usually discharged by the occupier putting up warning signs or making efforts to discourage a trespasser from running the risk. Therefore in the usual case, it is sufficient for a social landlord to put up signs on empty properties saying 'Danger. Keep Out'. This should be sufficient to discharge the occupier's duty towards adult trespassers.

If the danger is serious, or the landlord is aware that there are children in the area who tend to play in empty houses, it may be necessary for the landlord to board up the property or employ a watchman to warn children off where the danger is particularly severe. In any case, an empty property should be kept secure as it is foreseeable that a child may stray off the street into an empty property and injure him- or herself.

Where a trespasser knows the risk involved and yet runs it anyway, the occupier is not liable for any injury which he or she sustains.

Case report

The Birkenhead Corporation had a programme of slum clearance and was in the process of compulsorily acquiring a property to demolish it and replace it with new houses. The corporation had served a 'notice of entry' on the owner and her tenant, giving 14 days for the tenant to leave the property and offering alternative accommodation. The tenant informed the corporation that she would make her own arrangements and would soon move. The tenant left, but the corporation failed to board up the property as was its normal practice. Vandals broke down the front door and removed the glass from a second floor window.

A 4-year-old child wandered from a playground into the house and fell 30 feet from that window, suffering severe brain damage. The Court of Appeal held that the corporation, and not the owner, was the occupier of the property. It had the immediate right of control once the tenant had left as a result of the service of the notice of entry. The corporation should have known that the house was empty as the tenant had told an officer that she would shortly be leaving and its officers were also securing other houses in the area and must have observed that it was empty. It was therefore under a duty to protect the child from the danger of trespassing in the property by securing it against infant trespassers and was liable for her injuries. *Harris v Birkenhead Corporation and another* (1976)

Liability to those not on the premises

A social landlord's liability to those not on its premises for injury sustained as a result of the state of the premises or activities carried on there depends on whether it has parted with possession of the premises or is itself the occupier.

When landlord parts with possession

Negligence

Under the ordinary rules of negligence, a social landlord is liable if it causes defects in the premises which are likely to cause harm to others, whether on or off the premises, and harm is indeed caused. This liability for works done to the premises is preserved even when the premises are let (see discussion of DPA 1972, s. 3 above). Where premises are let on a licence, the landlord also may be liable for damage caused as a result of defects about which it ought to know even though they were not caused by it.

The statutory duty of care imposed by section 4 of DPA 1972 (see 34–35 above) also extends to those who might reasonably be expected to be affected by defects in the premises. This can clearly include people who are not on the premises such as neighbours and passers-by.

Nuisance

In law, nuisance is the unreasonable interference with another person's enjoyment of his or her property. An example is where a social landlord's premises have a defective drainpipe so that water floods over the neighbour's garden during heavy rain. It is usually the occupier of the property who is liable for nuisance, but there are exceptions.

The landlord is liable if it created the nuisance. So, for example, where the landlord does works to the premises which result in persistent flooding of a neighbour's premises or the recurrent escape of smoke over a neighbour's garden, it is liable as the creator of the nuisance. The landlord is also liable for a nuisance where:

- it knew or ought to have known about the nuisance before the letting; or
- it has covenanted to repair or has the right to enter and repair, and the nuisance is caused by the premises being out of repair (see also DPA 1972, s. 4 at pp. 34–35 above).

Generally social landlords are not liable for nuisance created by their tenants (*Smith v Scott* (1973)), even where the tenant is known by the landlord to be undesirable and highly likely to cause a nuisance to his or her neighbours (see C. Hunter and K. Bretherton, *Anti-social Behaviour* (Arden's Housing Library, 1998), ch. 2). A social landlord is liable, however, if it can be said to have authorised the nuisance, for example by letting the premises for a purpose which, in itself, constitutes a nuisance. Thus a local authority was liable in nuisance where it let land for go-karting as the nuisance was an inevitable consequence of that activity.

When landlord is the occupier

Where a social landlord is itself the occupier of premises, it is liable for injury caused to those not on the premises under the normal principles of negligence and nuisance outlined above. Therefore, the premises must be kept safe to avoid harm being caused to others, and must be kept in such state as to avoid nuisance to neighbours. Nuisance includes foul smells, vermin and blocked drains which cause flooding.

Liability for actions of trespassers

There are two main circumstances in which an occupier is liable for the acts of trespassers.

First, where the occupier creates a potentially hazardous situation on his or her land and it is foreseeable that trespassers will enter onto the premises and set off a train of events leading to damage to others' property or causes injury to others, the occupier is liable unless he or she takes reasonable care to secure the premises against entry by trespassers. For example, where highly flammable materials were stored in premises where there was a history of vandalism, including attempts to start fires, of which the occupier was or ought to have been aware, the occupier was under a duty to secure the premises against entry by vandals, if necessary by employing security guards (*Smith v Littlewoods Ltd* (1987)).

Secondly, where nuisance is created by the activities of trespassers on the occupier's land to the knowledge of the occupier and he or she does nothing to abate the nuisance, he or she may be said to be liable for 'adopting the nuisance'.

The occupier therefore has a duty to act to abate nuisance on his or her land. This may involve removing items which are causing the nuisance (e.g. items blocking a drain which is causing flooding), securing the premises, or even evicting the trespassers.

Case reports

The defendants' church was the subject of wide scale vandalism. On an inspection by the owners it was apparent that small fires had been lit by vandals inside the church. A local authority officer had reported that it should be demolished since it constituted a serious fire hazard. The owners failed to take the precaution of securing the side door of the church through which the vandals had gained access. A fire was then started by vandals in the church which spread and damaged neighbouring buildings. The church owners were held liable as they had failed to take reasonable precautions to prevent access. *Thomas Graham & Co v Church of Scotland General Trustees* (1982)

Page Motors conducted a car sales business on land adjacent to land owned by Epsom and Ewell BC which was squatted by gypsies. The local authority was aware of the gypsies' presence and provided them with basic sanitary facilities. The gypsies burned rubbish and rubber causing acrid smoke, obstructed access to Page Motors' premises, failed to control their animals which attacked customers, and did other acts which caused both customers and suppliers to be afraid to visit the premises, resulting in a loss of turnover. In 1974, the local authority commenced various proceedings to evict the gypsies but the possession orders were not enforced as a result of pressure from the county council and central government as there was nowhere else for the gypsies to go. An alternative site was provided in 1978 and the gypsies moved on.

The Court of Appeal held that the local authority, as owner of the land on which the gypsies were causing a nuisance and knowing of the nuisance, had a duty to take such steps as were reasonable to end the nuisance within a reasonable time. What was a reasonable time would depend on the circumstances in the case, including the broader issues such as the problems of finding an alternative site and the political pressure from the county council and central government. However, even taking this into account the local authority should have dealt with the matter sooner and so was liable for damages from the beginning of 1975. *Page Motors Ltd v Epsom and Ewell BC* (1981)

Mr Lippiatt and Mr Febry were tenant farmers. South Gloucestershire Council owned a strip of land next to their farms on the edge of the road. The council allowed travellers to occupy the land between 1991 and 1994, when it evicted them. The farmers complained that, during this period, the travellers had trespassed onto their land and done various harmful things, such as leaving rubbish and excrement, tethering their own livestock there, stealing timber and fences, and damaging a wall and crops. They sued the council, alleging that these acts constituted a nuisance. In the county court the judge struck out the case, saying that it did not give rise to a cause of action as all the alleged damage had occurred on the farmers' land, and not the council's.

The Court of Appeal allowed the farmers' appeal. It held that the owner-occupier of land (in this case the council) could be liable in nuisance for the unlawful activities of his licensees or persons based on his land even where the acts complained of were committed off his land. Thus, where the nuisance consisted of repeated acts on the victim's land, which took place to the owner's knowledge and interfered with the victim's enjoyment of his own land, it was arguable that a nuisance had been committed. The case was remitted to the judge for trial of the facts.
Lippiatt v South Gloucestershire Council (1999)

Key points

- An occupier is the person who has a sufficient degree of physical control over the premises to be able to ensure their safety.

Where the landlord has parted with possession of the premises:

- It is liable for disrepair to the premises which falls within any repairing obligations.
- It is liable for any damage or injury caused by defects in the property which were created by its own negligence.
- It is liable for defective works which it has carried out to the premises which cause injury or damage to property.
- Where it lets the property on a tenancy, it is liable for any defects which it has a right or obligation to repair and which cause injury or damage to property or to any person who might reasonably be expected to be affected by the defects, including those not on the premises.

- The landlord is liable to those not on the premises under the normal principles of nuisance.
- The landlord is not usually liable for the nuisance created by its tenants.

Where the landlord is an occupier

- The landlord owes its visitors a duty to take such care as is reasonable in the circumstances to see that the visitors and their property are reasonably safe in using the premises for the purposes for which they are invited or permitted to be there.
- The landlord must be prepared for children to be less careful than adults.
- Visitors in the course of business are expected to guard against any risks which are normal aspects of their business.
- The landlord owes a limited duty to trespassers where it knows or ought to know of a danger on the property and the proximity of trespassers to the danger and it is a risk against which the landlord may reasonably be expected to offer the trespasser some protection.
- The landlord must take reasonable steps to ensure that the state of its premises are such that they do not create a nuisance or cause injury to those not on the premises.
- In limited circumstances, an occupier is liable for the actions of trespassers.

Part II

Occupiers' Rights

5.

Classes of Occupation

Tenants / Licensees / Trespassers

In order to use empty property effectively and to manage the use of all their property, social landlords must be familiar with the different sorts of interests which they can grant in property and the different legal rights which accompany them. Different interests or classes of occupation carry with them different amounts of legal protection. Most significantly this affects the ease and method of obtaining possession against the occupier. It is therefore important to be able to distinguish clearly between different types of occupier.

Colloquial expressions are often used to classify types of occupier. These expressions are not, however, recognised legal terminology. As a result, they can be misleading in describing what protection an occupier has. For example, the term 'unauthorised occupier', while current in housing management, has no recognised legal meaning. It is not, in itself, descriptive of the rights that such an occupier may have. Similarly, while the term 'squatter' is universally understood, it is not a term which is often used by the courts.

There are four main types of occupation:

- owner-occupation (which includes long leases);
- occupation under a tenancy;
- occupation pursuant to a licence; and
- trespass.

Owner-occupation is beyond the scope of this book; while tenants may become owner-occupiers of property originally owned by social landlords by way of the 'right to buy' (see J. Henderson, *Rights to Buy and Acquire* (Arden's Housing Library, 1997)), social landlords are not usually concerned in the management of its occupation. However, the other types of occupation and how they are created are detailed below.

Tenants

There are four basic conditions that must be fulfilled for the existence of a tenancy. First, there must be a landlord and a tenant. The landlord can be the owner of the property or can itself be a tenant. There is no requirement for the tenant to know who the landlord is as all dealings can be done through an agent. In the case of social landlords, the parties are usually known to each other and there is no dispute over this condition. Where there are two or more landlords or tenants, they are known as 'joint landlords' and 'joint tenants'.

Secondly, there must be identifiable premises. These can be as little as one room.

Thirdly, there must be an identifiable period for which the premises are let. This can be a fixed term (e.g. a tenancy for six months). Where no fixed term is specified, a tenancy can be periodic (e.g. from week to week). Where the other conditions for a tenancy are satisfied and there is no fixed term but rent is payable in relation to a particular period, a periodic tenancy is created. The period of the tenancy will be the period in relation to which rent is payable.

Fourthly, there must be a grant of exclusive possession. This means that the tenant can exclude everyone else from the premises, *including the landlord*. It is this aspect which allows a tenant to call the premises his or her home. A single occupier usually has exclusive possession unless the landlord needs to gain access to the premises on a regular basis to provide services or where the landlord genuinely needs to reserve the right to move the occupier from one room to another (an example being hostel occupation). Where there is sharing of premises, unless there is a joint tenancy, the occupiers do not have exclusive possession of the whole premises. They might, however, have exclusive possession of a smaller part of the premises, such as a bedroom, while sharing the rest of the premises.

Once these conditions are fulfilled, there is a tenancy regardless of what the arrangement has been called by the parties unless it falls within one of the exceptions dealt with below. There are many so-called licence agreements which are in fact tenancies. It is interesting to note that the payment of rent is not essential for the existence of a tenancy, although it strongly suggests that a tenancy has been created.

Exceptions

These are as follows.

No intention to create legal relations

No tenancy is created where there is no intention to create legal relations. This can be for a number of reasons, such as a family relationship between the occupier and the landlord, or where the occupier is permitted to live in the property as an act of charity or generosity. Another example is where a landlord taking possession proceedings against an occupier who has no right to be in the property accepts rent by mistake; this is not usually taken to result in the creation of a tenancy as there would not be the required intention on the part of the landlord (*Westminster City Council v Basson* (1990)).

Landlord lacks capacity to grant tenancy

A tenancy can only be granted by a person with either the freehold or the leasehold title to the premises. This means that a licensee cannot create a tenancy of the property. A principle has been developed, however, by which a person who purports to grant a tenancy without having the capacity to do so may be bound by that grant as against the occupier. This means that a tenancy exists between the occupier and the grantor, together with all the rights and statutory protection that go with a tenancy. This is called a 'tenancy by estoppel'. The true owner or leaseholder is not bound by the occupier's rights.

Case report

London and Quadrant Housing Trust had licences of property from Lambeth LBC for providing short-life accommodation (see also Chap. 3). Mr Bruton, knowing that the Housing Trust lacked the capacity to grant a tenancy, signed a 'licence agreement' with the Housing Trust to occupy a self-contained flat in one of the properties. This amounted to a grant of exclusive possession. The Court of Appeal held that it was clear to Mr Bruton that the Housing Trust did not have the capacity to grant a tenancy. Not only that, but it had made it clear that it was only granting a licence. Despite the fact that all the conditions for a tenancy were met, the court held that Mr Bruton only had a licence.

The House of Lords reversed this decision. The agreement granted exclusive possession; the Housing Trust had reserved rights of entry, which was incompatible with the grant of a licence. The Housing Trust's lack of capacity was irrelevant. Accordingly, Mr Bruton had a tenancy. *Bruton v London and Quadrant Housing Trust* (1999)

Legal relations other than tenancy

The most common example of this exception is where there is an agreement for occupation of tied accommodation. This is accommodation given to an employee of the landlord. Where it is a requirement in an employment contract that the employee occupy certain premises and the occupation of those premises materially assists in the performance of his or her duties, then he or she is a 'service occupier'. Even if he or she pays rent and all the conditions of a tenancy are met, he or she is in fact a licensee. He or she has no right to stay in the premises after the employment contract ends.

Where there is no requirement in the employment contract for the employee to occupy the premises, unless occupation of the premises is essential for the performance of his or her duties, he or she is a tenant and has statutory protection.

Creation of a tenancy

A tenancy is usually created by a written agreement, signed by both parties. A tenancy for a fixed term of more than three years must be made by a deed. Otherwise, a tenancy can be created orally. It is advisable, however, to make sure that tenancies are in writing for two reasons: first, so that both parties have proof of the tenancy's existence, and secondly to ensure that any relevant terms and conditions of the tenancy are included. Where a social landlord produces terms and conditions in a separate booklet, the document which the tenant signs must refer to these conditions and specifically incorporate them into the tenancy.

While payment of rent is not essential for a tenancy to exist, it is one of the most common ways in which a tenancy is created. Where a landlord gives a person exclusive occupation of premises and charges or accepts money from him or her on a periodic basis, it is likely that a tenancy has been created. Landlords therefore must be careful about accepting rent from people who are not their tenants. In these circumstances it should be made clear that acceptance of a payment is not intended to create a tenancy.

Local authorities need to take care not to create tenancies inadvertently as any grant of a secure tenancy is treated as an allocation and must be in accordance with the authority's housing allocations policy (HA 1996, s. 167(8)).

Licensees

A licence is a grant of permission to do something (e.g. to live in premises). Where an occupier has permission to live in, but is not a tenant of, the premises, he or she is a licensee. This is because either the arrangement falls within one of the exceptions to a tenancy or the occupier does not have exclusive possession of the premises. In the private sector, this comes about most commonly when the occupier is a lodger. In the context of social housing, licences are usually granted of hostel accommodation where the landlord needs access to the rooms to provide services, such as cleaning. The occupier does not, therefore, have exclusive possession.

Contractual licences

A contractual licence is created where there is a contract between the parties involving permission to be on premises. Usually a contractual licence involves payment. There may be conditions for the use of the premises. There may be provision for how the licence is to be brought to an end. A contractual licence may look similar to a tenancy agreement in its terms, but it usually states that the agreement is a licence and does not grant exclusive possession.

Bare licences

A bare licence is a simple grant of permission to be on land. There will not be any payment or any other conditions.

Creation of licences

A licence is usually created by express agreement, either orally or in writing. As with a tenancy, where a contractual licence is entered into, it is wise to have a written agreement so that any terms can be proved. In circumstances where no tenancy can be granted, the payment of money in return for accommodation results in a contractual licence.

As a bare licence relies merely on permission being granted for occupation, it is not essential that there should be an express agreement. Permission can be implied from the landlord's conduct. Mere failure to bring possession proceedings against an unauthorised occupier should not be interpreted by a court as granting permission, although it could be different if the landlord appeared to acquiesce in such occupation. This might be done by requiring the occupier to carry out repairs at the premises or by corresponding with the occupier in terms which implied that he or she had permission to be on the premises. When housing officers discover that persons are in occupation of premises without the landlord's express agreement, they should quickly make it clear to the occupiers that the landlord has not given them permission to occupy the premises.

Trespassers

A trespasser is anyone who is on land without permission to be there. This includes anyone who has entered the land without permission in the first place or who has remained on the land after whatever permission he or she had has expired. Someone who has a licence to do certain things on premises can become a trespasser merely by exceeding the terms of the licence. Different types of trespassers have different amounts of protection.

Outright trespassers

These are trespassers who enter land without permission. Where they enter land in order to live there, they are also known as 'squatters'. These people have the least protection from the law.

Holding over

'Holding over' is where someone has had a tenancy or licence of premises and remains after the tenancy or licence ends and a reasonable period has expired for that person to leave. As soon as he or she holds over, he or she becomes a trespasser. Where HA 1985 or 1988 applies to the tenancy (see further pp. 59–63 below), the tenancy or licence does not come to an end until ordered by the court. In those cases, the tenant or licensee does not become a trespasser until after the date ordered by the court for possession, even though the landlord no longer wants him or her on the premises.

A common situation arises when

- an occupier was let into premises by a tenant or licensee, but
- remains after the tenancy or licence has been brought to an end; and
- the ex-tenant or licensee has him- or herself left the property.

This can also be considered as a kind of holding over. An example of this is key-selling. It is not uncommon for tenants, particularly of local authority property, who wish to move to sell the keys to someone who is looking for accommodation rather than returning them to the authority. While this is obviously against the terms of the tenancy agreement, it is still necessary to terminate the original tenancy before taking action against the occupiers. If the occupiers remain once the tenancy has been brought to an end, they are also holding over.

Key points

- The four categories of occupation are owner-occupation, tenancy, licence and trespass.
- A landlord who grants exclusive possession of premises for a term (which may be fixed or periodic) grants a tenancy unless the situation falls within an exception.
- The exceptions are where there is no intention to create legal relations, where the landlord lacks capacity to grant a tenancy and where the grant is explicable because of some other relationship between the landlord and the occupier.

- Rent is not an essential element, although it is strong evidence, of a tenancy.
- Tenancies for less than three years do not have to be in writing, although it is advisable.
- A licence is a grant of permission to occupy premises.
- Licences usually arise because either the landlord does not grant exclusive possession or the occupation falls within one of the exceptions to a tenancy.
- Trespassers may have entered the property without permission or remained on the property when any right they had has been brought to an end.

6.

Statutory Protection and Security

Tenants / Licensees / Trespassers / Flowcharts outlining security

Once it has been established whether an occupier is a tenant, licensee or trespasser, it is necessary to assess what statutory protection he or she enjoys. This affects what a landlord must do to regain possession of the property and how straightforward it will be. This chapter sets out the different kinds of statutory protection and to whom they apply.

The main sources of statutory protection are HA 1985 (secure tenants and licensees), HA 1988 (assured tenants), and the Protection from Eviction Act (PEA) 1977 (protection for tenants and licensees with no security). For a more general discussion of the Housing Acts, see A. Dymond, *Security of Tenure* (2nd edn, Arden's Housing Library, 2000)).

One aspect which often causes confusion is that occupiers protected by the Housing Acts are said to have 'security of tenure'. This includes both secure *and* assured tenants, as well as secure licensees. Similarly, occupiers with no statutory protection are often called 'non-secure', meaning that they are neither secure tenants or licensees nor assured tenants.

Tenants

Most residential tenants are protected by HA 1985 or 1988 unless they are specifically excluded. Tenancies granted by local authorities are governed by HA 1985 and are called 'secure tenancies'; tenancies granted by most other social landlords are governed by HA 1988 and are called 'assured tenancies'. An exception to this is co-operative housing associations. Where these are registered with the Housing Corporation, tenancies granted by them have no security whatsoever. Where they are not registered, any tenancies they granted before 15 January 1989 are secure tenancies.

Conditions for secure tenancy

A tenancy under which a dwelling-house is let as a separate dwelling is secure at any time when:

- the landlord is a local authority, new town corporation, housing action trust, urban development corporation or the Development Board for Rural Wales (the 'landlord condition': HA 1985, s. 80); and
- the tenant is an individual and occupies the premises as his or her only or principal home (the 'tenant condition': HA 1985, s. 81); and
- the tenancy does not come within any of the statutory exceptions (see further pp. 60–61 below).

Conditions for assured tenancy

A tenancy under which a dwelling-house is let as a separate dwelling is an assured tenancy at any time when:

- the tenant is an individual and occupies the dwelling-house as his or her only or principal home; and
- the tenancy does not come within any of the statutory exceptions (see further pp. 61–62 below).

Assured shorthold tenancy

Assured shorthold tenancies are a sub-category of assured tenancies. Before 23 February 1997, to create an assured shorthold tenancy, it was necessary to serve a notice on the tenant under section 20 of HA 1988 before the tenancy was entered into. From 23 February 1997, however, all new assured tenancies are assured shorthold tenancies unless the landlord serves a notice on the tenant that the tenancy is to be an assured tenancy.

Occupation as only or principal home

This is the most important condition, and failure to comply with it is the most common way by which tenants of social landlords lose their security. (For a full discussion of the other conditions, i.e. whether premises are a dwelling-house or let as a separate dwelling, see A. Dymond, *Security of Tenure* (Arden's Housing Library, 2nd edn, 1999), ch. 4.)

Whether someone is living in premises as their only or principal home is a matter of fact or degree. For example, a tenant may work away from home for long periods. The tenant's cultural background may also need to be taken into account; he or she may occasionally spend long periods abroad visiting relatives, or may have a more fluid living pattern and stay in other family members' homes whilst retaining his or her own only or principal home. Housing officers need to be aware of such lifestyles.

Tenants can also lose their statutory protection by subletting. These issues are dealt with more fully in Chapter 8.

Exceptions from security

These are found in Schedule 1 to HA 1985 for secure tenancies and Schedule 1 to HA 1988 for assured tenancies. They are dealt with in detail in A. Dymond, *Security of Tenure* (2nd edn, Arden's Housing Library, 2000), ch. 3.

Tenancies which cannot be secure tenancies

The main categories of tenancies within Schedule 1 to HA 1985 which cannot be secure are as follows:

- long leases (para. 1)

- introductory tenancies (para. 1A)
- employment tenancies (para. 2)
- development land (para. 3)
- accommodation for homeless persons (para. 4)
- temporary accommodation for persons taking up accommodation in an area (para. 5)
- subleasing schemes for short-term accommodation (para. 6)
- temporary accommodation during works (para. 7)
- agricultural holdings (para. 8)
- licensed premises (para. 9)
- student lettings (para. 10)
- business tenancies (para. 11)
- almshouses (para. 12).

The exceptions which are likely to be most important and/or useful in the area covered by this book are development land, accommodation for homeless persons and accommodation during works. These are dealt with in Chapter 3 above.

A tenancy is also not secure if it has been granted by the local authority as a temporary expedient to someone who entered the dwelling-house or any other land as a trespasser (HA 1985, s. 79(4)).

Tenancies which cannot be assured tenancies

The categories of tenancy within Schedule 1 to HA 1988 which cannot be assured tenancies are as follows:

- tenancies granted before 15 January 1989 (para. 1)
- tenancies of dwelling-houses with high rateable values (para. 2)
- tenancies at no or low rent (para. 3)
- business tenancies (para. 4)
- licensed premises (para. 5)
- agricultural tenancies (paras 6 and 7)
- student lettings (para. 8)
- holiday lettings (para. 9)
- resident landlords (para. 10)
- Crown tenancies (para. 11)

- local authority tenancies (para. 12)
- secure, housing association and Rent Act tenancies (para. 13).

Statutory protection for tenants with no security

Tenants who fall outside the HA 1985 and HA 1988 provisions do not lose all statutory protection. They are protected by PEA 1977 unless they have what are known as 'excluded tenancies'.

The PEA 1977 makes it unlawful to evict a tenant whose tenancy has come to an end without first obtaining a court order (s. 3(1)). Where such order has been obtained, it is still necessary to obtain a warrant of possession and for the bailiffs to carry out the eviction (*Haniff v Robinson* (1993)). If a landlord carries out an eviction without a court order, it, and any of its officers involved in the eviction, commits an offence which is punishable with a fine or up to two years' imprisonment (s. 1). The PEA 1977 also lays down requirements for the form and length of notices to quit (see pp. 73–74 below).

Tenancies which are excluded from the protection of PEA 1977 are set out in section 3A. Some are not specifically relevant for social landlords, such as that where the tenant shares accommodation with his or her landlord. The most relevant exclusions are as follows:

- A tenancy granted as a temporary expedient to a trespasser (s. 3A(6)). Thus a social landlord which finds trespassers in one of its properties can offer the trespasser a tenancy or licence of alternative premises as a temporary expedient, and PEA 1977 will not apply.
- A tenancy under which no rent is payable and for which the tenant makes no payment in kind (s. 3A(7)(b)).
- A tenancy which confers rights of occupation in a hostel within the meaning of HA 1985 which is provided by a local authority, a housing trust which is a charity or an RSL or one of various other specified public bodies (s. 3A(8)).

Where a tenancy is excluded, there is no requirement on a landlord to obtain a court order to gain possession of the property. It is not always cut and dried, however, whether a tenancy *is* in fact excluded. The penalties for evicting someone when in fact a court order was required are very severe. Not only is it a criminal offence, but the occupier may bring a civil action for unlawful eviction, in which damages can be high. A landlord should also be aware of the possibility of committing an offence under section 6 of the Criminal Law Act 1977 (for which see Chap. 13). It is therefore usually a good idea to go to court for a possession order rather than simply to change the locks.

Licensees

The amount of protection given to licensees depends on the identity of the landlord. Licensees of local authorities may have security of tenure under HA 1985. The HA 1988, however, does not give any protection to licensees. This means that the licensees of other social landlords (where the licence is granted after 15 January 1989) are not protected by HA 1988.

Local authority licensees

Under HA 1985, some licensees are treated as if they are tenants (s. 79(3)). They are given security of tenure and are known as 'secure licensees'. A licensee can still be secure even though he or she pays nothing for his or her right of occupation. The same exceptions to security apply as they do to tenants (see above).

To qualify for security, a licence must give the occupier the right to exclusive possession of premises which he or she occupies as a separate dwelling. This means in effect that security only applies to licences where either (a) there is no agreement as to the term for which the right to occupy has been granted and there is no periodic payment of a licence fee, or (b) all the conditions for a tenancy are present but one of the exceptions to the grant of a tenancy is present (see above). Examples of this are where the local authority allows a person into occupation of property pending the signing of a tenancy agreement or where there is no intention of creating legal relations. The latter may be demonstrated if no charge is made for the accommodation, although this is not conclusive.

The mere fact that an agreement is a licence does not, therefore, exempt it from security. The landlord must legitimately retain some control over the premises. Thus, a local authority must genuinely have a requirement to be able to enter the property without restrictions or to move the occupiers from one room to another. This can be to perform services, but would also apply to a hostel where, for proper management purposes, the occupants can be moved between rooms.

Case report

Mr Clarke had a licence of a room in a hostel owned by the City of Westminster. The hostel was used to house homeless single men, many of whom had personality disorders or physical disabilities; some had been discharged from hospital or from prison. There was a resident warden and a team of social workers. Mr Clarke had been placed in the hostel as part of a rehabilitation programme. The licence conditions included a prohibition on allowing persons to stay overnight and on causing a nuisance to other occupants, and a requirement to be in the accommodation by 11pm. The council also reserved the right to change the room provided to Mr Clarke or to require him to share accommodation.

The council served notice to quit on Mr Clarke, who argued that he had been granted a secure licence which could only be brought to an end if there were grounds. The House of Lords decided that, on the special facts of this case, the agreement did not give Mr Clarke exclusive possession of his room. Taking into account the nature of the accommodation, the object of the council in providing temporary accommodation to vulnerable people and the administrative necessity for the council to control the use of all the rooms in the hostel, the council had retained possession of Mr Clarke's room. To be secure a licence had to confer exclusive possession. Mr Clarke's licence had been properly terminated by notice to quit. *Westminster City Council v Clark* (1992)

Another important exception to the grant of a licence by a local authority resulting in a secure licence can be found in section 79(4) of HA 1985. When an occupier enters premises as a trespasser and the authority later grants him or her a licence of the premises as a temporary expedient, that licence cannot be secure. Further, if the authority later offers the occupier another licence of the same premises or even a licence of different premises, that licence is not secure as long as there is some connection between the grant of the licence and the original trespass. The local authority must make sure that the person was, in fact, a trespasser from the beginning before granting a licence on the basis that it will not be secure. An occupier who was allowed into the property by a previous tenant and then remains after the termination of the tenancy does not come under this section and so any licence granted to him or her is secure.

Licensees with no security of tenure

As stated above, licensees are not protected by HA 1988. Thus, any licence granted by a non-local authority social landlord has no security. These licensees, and those local authority licensees who are not secure, may, however, be protected by PEA 1977, which applies to licensees in the same way as to tenants. The same exclusions apply (see above). This means that bare licensees are not protected as they do not make any payment for their right to occupy accommodation.

Trespassers

Trespassers are not protected by the Housing Acts. In some circumstances, however, they may be protected by PEA 1977.

Also relevant are the provisions of section 6 of the Criminal Law Act 1977, which make it an offence to use violence to secure entry to residential premises when there is someone in occupation who is opposed to the entry (see also Chap. 13).

Outright trespassers

Occupiers who entered property as trespassers have no statutory protection save for the provisions of section 6 of the Criminal Law Act 1977. Subject to that, landlords may take possession themselves without going to court, usually by changing the locks. Given the risk, however, that the landlord may inadvertently have granted the occupiers a licence which has not been brought to an end and the penalties for not obtaining a court order for possession when one is required, it is wise to issue court proceedings. There is a quick procedure specifically designed for recovery of land which is occupied by trespassers; this is found in the Civil Procedure Rules, Schedule 2, CCR Order 24 (see generally Chap. 9).

Holding over

Former tenants and licensees as discussed at pp. 55–56 above are protected by PEA 1977 unless they are excluded. The following therefore deals with the position where the previous tenant or licensee allowed persons into the property who have remained after the termination of the tenancy or licence. Their protection depends on what interest they themselves were granted by the ex-tenant or licensee.

Subtenants

A subtenancy can only be granted by a person who is a tenant (the 'head tenant'). The position of subtenants depends on whether their subtenancy was lawful. A subtenancy is unlawful where:

- the head tenancy is a secure tenancy and the subtenancy is of the whole of the property; or
- in any other case, the landlord has not given consent for the grant of a subtenancy; or
- the subtenancy is in breach of the conditions of the tenancy agreement.

In the second two situations, the landlord can waive the illegality by accepting rent from the tenant with full knowledge of the subtenancy. If that happens, the subtenancy is considered to be legal.

Where the subtenancy is a lawful assured tenancy when the head tenancy is brought to an end, the subtenant has an assured tenancy directly from the head landlord. The original tenant simply drops out of the picture. In any other case, when the landlord brings the head tenancy to an end, the subtenancy comes to an end as well. Where the subtenancy is lawful, the occupier is protected by the terms of PEA 1977 (as long as the head tenancy is not itself excluded) and the landlord must obtain a court order to gain possession. This is because PEA 1977 only protects those who are 'lawfully residing in the premises or part of them at the termination of the former tenancy [or licence]' (s. 3(2)). When the subtenancy is unlawful, therefore, PEA 1977 does not apply.

Licensees

There is usually no restriction on a tenant or licensee allowing persons onto the premises. Such a person is a licensee of the tenant or licensee and is lawfully on the premises. Those to whom the keys of premises have been sold by the tenant are usually considered as licensees of the tenant. Despite the fact that it is not lawful to sell the keys, this in itself does not make the occupation by the licensee unlawful. All such persons therefore have the protection of PEA 1977 as long as the head tenancy or licence is not itself excluded.

Flowcharts outlining security

The following flowcharts assume that the occupier is an individual (or individuals) and that the premises are a dwelling-house.

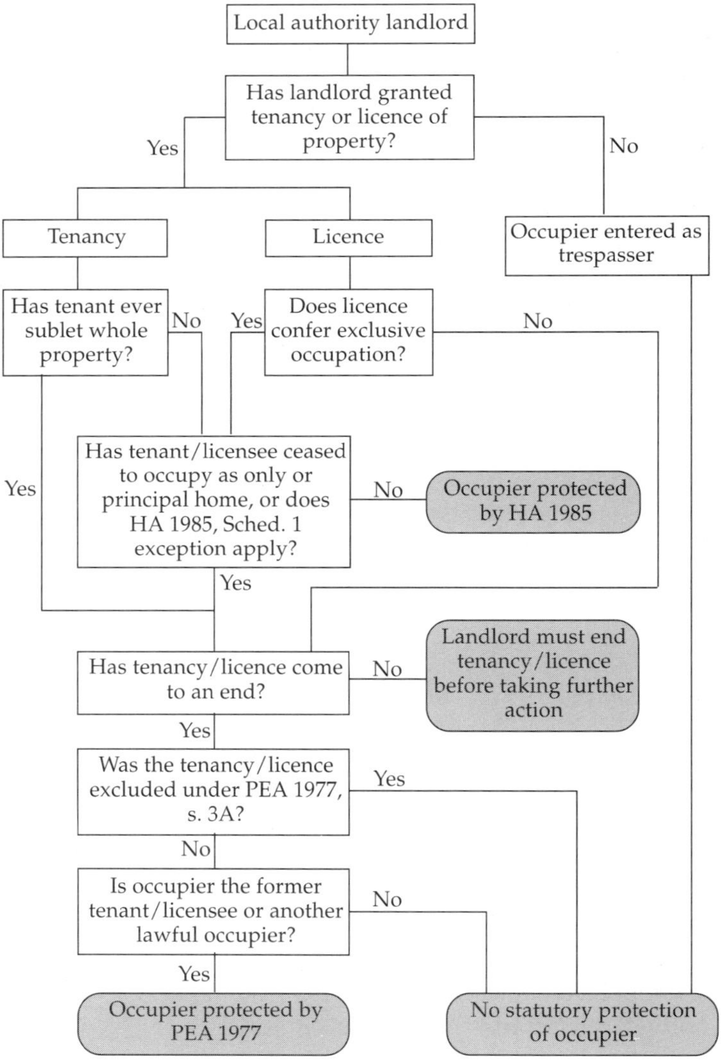

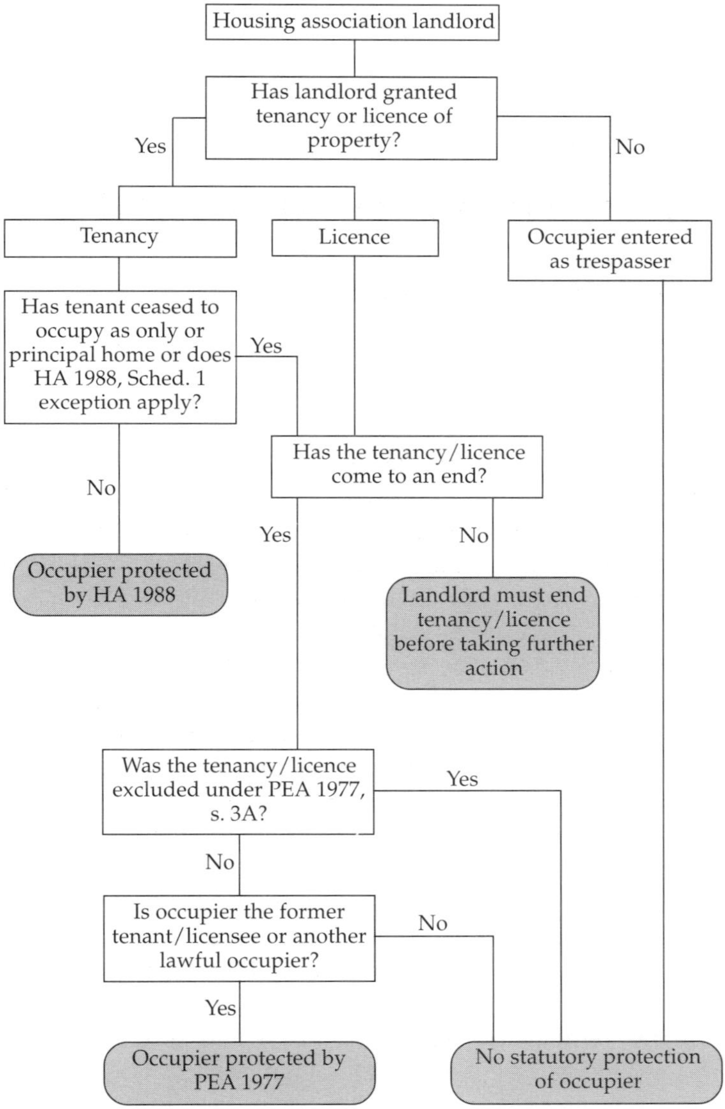
Housing association landlord
Has landlord granted tenancy or licence of property?
Yes
No
Tenancy
Licence
Occupier entered as trespasser
Has tenant ceased to occupy as only or principal home or does HA 1988, Sched. 1 exception apply?
Yes
No
Has the tenancy/licence come to an end?
Occupier protected by HA 1988
Yes
No
Landlord must end tenancy/licence before taking further action
Was the tenancy/licence excluded under PEA 1977, s. 3A?
Yes
No
Is occupier the former tenant/licensee or another lawful occupier?
No
Yes
Occupier protected by PEA 1977
No statutory protection of occupier

7.

Termination of Rights of Occupation

Termination of tenancies / Termination of licences

Possession proceedings can only be brought by someone immediately entitled to possession. Therefore, before a landlord can recover possession of premises, it must first terminate any rights of occupation it may have granted. Where an occupier is the tenant or licensee of the landlord, then it is this right which must be brought to an end. Where the occupier is someone with whom the landlord has never had any connection, the landlord must terminate any tenancy or licence of the property which is still continuing. For example, where the occupier is a person let in by the previous tenant who has since left, the landlord must terminate the tenant's interest before he can bring possession proceedings against the occupier. This is because, until the tenant's interest is brought to an end, only the tenant has an immediate right of occupation.

This chapter looks at the ways different kinds of occupation can be brought to an end. This depends not only on whether the occupier is a tenant, licensee or trespasser, but also on the kind of statutory protection he or she enjoys.

Termination of tenancies

The procedure for termination depends on whether the tenancy has security. The procedure for secure and assured tenancies is beyond the scope of this book so an outline only is given (see further A. Dymond, *Security of Tenure* (Arden's Housing Library, 2nd edn, 1999)). When dealing with unauthorised occupiers, however, social landlords are often in the position of having to bring the most recent tenancy to an end. Commonly the tenant has moved out, ceasing to occupy the premises as his or her only or principal home, and may have lost his or her security (see pp. 58–60 above). This section therefore deals in more detail with termination of non-secure tenancies.

Tenancies with security

Secure tenancies

A secure tenancy can only be brought to an end by a court order. It comes to an end on the date specified in the order. Before a court can hear proceedings for possession, the landlord must serve a notice seeking possession under section 83 of HA 1985 which must specify the grounds on which possession is sought. The court can only make an order for possession if one of the statutory grounds is made out. In some cases the landlord must provide suitable alternative accommodation. In most cases the court must also be satisfied that it is reasonable to make an order. The court also has power to suspend the operation of the order on conditions.

Assured tenancies

Assured (though *not* shorthold—see below) tenancies require a similar procedure to secure tenancies. The relevant notice seeking possession is required by section 8 of HA 1988.

Assured shorthold tenancies

There is no requirement to prove any of the statutory grounds for possession where the tenancy is an assured shorthold. Where the tenancy is for a fixed term, it must have expired. The landlord must serve a notice under section 21 of HA 1988.

As long as the required procedures are followed, the court must order possession.

Non-secure tenancies

Where the Housing Acts do not apply, termination of a tenancy is governed by the general law. The correct procedure for determining a tenancy depends on whether it is periodic or for a fixed term. Most tenancies granted by social landlords are periodic.

Fixed-term tenancies

There are three main ways for a fixed-term tenancy to come to an end:

- expiry of the fixed term; or
- by operation of a break clause; or
- by the landlord forfeiting the tenancy.

The simplest way for a fixed-term tenancy to come to an end is by its expiry, when the tenancy automatically ends. Once expired, the landlord need do nothing more to end the tenancy.

The other means of ending a tenancy depend on the terms of the tenancy agreement. Some fixed-term tenancies contain a 'break clause', which allows the landlord (and usually also the tenant) to end the tenancy at a specified time part way through the term. The tenancy can only be ended on the date specified by the contract. How this right is to be exercised is stated in the contract and it is important to comply exactly with the contractual terms. It is usually done by serving a notice which states that the landlord (or tenant) wishes to exercise the right under the break clause. The notice should state the correct expiry date although, as long as it is clear to a reasonable person what is meant by the notice, a mistake over the date may not be fatal.

If there is no break clause, the landlord can still determine the tenancy part way through the term where rent is not being paid or there is a breach of some other obligation of the tenancy. This depends on there being a 'right of re-entry' specified in the agreement. Such provision allows the landlord to re-enter the property if the tenant falls into arrears or breaches any obligation. An example of such a phrase is:

> If the rent or any instalment or part thereof shall be in arrear for at least fourteen days after the same shall have become due (whether legally demanded or not) or if there shall be a breach of any of the agreements by the Tenant, the Landlord may re-enter on the Property and immediately thereupon the tenancy shall absolutely determine.

When the landlord exercises this right, it is said to be 'forfeiting' the tenancy. The detailed law of forfeiture is beyond the scope of this book (but see A. Dymond, *Security of Tenure* (2nd edn, above), pp. 61–66).

Periodic tenancies

In periodic tenancies, there is no agreement for the tenancy to come to an end at a particular time. Instead, occupation is referable to a period, usually being the period in respect of which rent is paid. For example, if rent is due every week, there is a weekly tenancy. If the landlord and the tenant do nothing, the tenancy automatically continues from week to week. If either party wants to end the tenancy, however, that party must give a notice to quit to the other, stating that it wants the tenancy to come to an end. As long as it is in the correct form and is properly served, the notice operates automatically to end the tenancy and cannot be retracted. So, if the tenant is thereafter allowed to remain in occupation, a new tenancy is created.

Length of notice

For a notice to quit to be operative, it must give the correct minimum period of notice. The correct period is usually the same as the period of the tenancy. There are two exceptions:

first, for yearly tenancies, the correct period is six months; secondly, the minimum notice period is 28 days (PEA 1977, s. 5)—thus for a weekly tenancy, the notice to quit must give 28 days' notice. The notice period must expire on the first or last day of a period of the tenancy, and runs from the time when the tenant or the landlord has actually been served.

Because it is important for a notice to quit to expire on the correct day, it is common (and advisable) for a notice to quit to contain a 'saving clause'. This requires the tenant to leave the premises 'on [*date*] or on that day next not less than four weeks from the service of this notice when a complete period of your tenancy shall expire'.

Example

Mr Brown has a tenancy of 25 Riverside from Norchester District Council under which he must pay rent every Monday. Mr Brown moves to Land's End and intends never to return to Riverside. To terminate his tenancy, the council needs to serve a notice to quit which expires on a Sunday or a Monday. Service must take place four weeks before the notice expires—that is on or before the Sunday four weeks before if it expires on Sunday and on or before the Monday four weeks before if it expires on Monday.

Form of the notice

A notice to quit must be in writing and must state unequivocally that the tenancy is to end. If the notice is served by the landlord, it must also contain some prescribed information. Most social landlords have their own standard forms of notices to quit which contain that information.

Service of the notice

The general rule is that a notice to quit must be served personally (i.e. it must be given directly into the hands of the tenant). Service is also sufficient if the notice is left at the property and the landlord can show that it came into the hands of the tenant, his wife or his servant in sufficient time to give the required period of notice to determine the tenancy. These days this would probably include the tenant's husband. So, where the notice to quit is put through the letterbox, if the tenant admits receipt of the notice in time, the notice can still be effective. If, however, there is no proof that it came to the tenant's attention, the court is unlikely to order possession.

There are limited exceptions to this rule. First, if the tenancy agreement provides that notices are sufficiently served if served at the property, service need not be personally on the tenant. Secondly, if the tenancy is in writing and 'requires' the service of a notice to quit to terminate the tenancy, the landlord can rely on the provisions of section 196 of the Law of Property Act (LPA) 1925. This provides that service is sufficient if the notice is (a) left at or sent by registered post to the tenant's last-known place of abode or business in the UK, or (b) left for the tenant at or fixed to the premises which are the subject of the tenancy.

Even where the landlord's standard conditions of tenancy contain a term which fulfils either of the above requirements, the landlord must be able to show that the term applies to the tenancy in question (i.e. such standard conditions must have been incorporated into the tenancy agreement). This is unlikely to have happened if the tenancy was created informally. It also shows the importance of keeping proper records so that there is documentary proof that the tenancy incorporated the standard conditions.

In most cases where there has been a management transfer, the court will be satisfied if the notice to quit is served on the new property. Strictly speaking, however, this does not prove receipt of the notice by the tenant. Usually the tenant is not a party to the possession proceedings and therefore is not present to give evidence. If there are concerns over whether service can be proved, the tenant should be made a party and asked to give evidence about the receipt of the notice to quit.

The main problem with the strict rules on service of notices is that of absent tenants. Obviously it is usually very difficult to serve them personally. If the housing officer's enquiries reveal the tenant's new address, the notice to quit should be served personally on the tenant at that property. If personal service is impractical, the notice should be served by recorded delivery post. If it is successfully delivered, it is likely that the court will infer on the balance of probabilities that service has taken place. However, this is not the same as personal service and the court may not accept that the landlord has proved proper service.

Where no address is known there is no possibility of serving the tenant personally. Here, the only chance of determining the tenancy by notice to quit is where section 196 of LPA 1925 applies to the tenancy, thus enabling the service of the notice at the premises. If section 196 does not apply, it is not possible to determine the tenancy by notice to quit except by finding the tenant. Social landlords should consider the use of inquiry agents in such circumstances.

Where the tenant has died, there are slightly different rules for servicing a notice to quit, as set out in Chapter 8.

Case report

Mr D succeeded to his mother's tenancy with the Enfield LBC. A suspended possession order was made against him on the ground of rent arrears. Miss S moved into the flat with him, but he later moved out. An agreement was made between Mr D and the council for repayment of the arrears. It was conceded in the county court that this created a new tenancy (although that would probably not now be the case). This new tenancy did not incorporate the council's standard conditions of tenancy which included a term that 'the tenancy may be ended by the tenant giving to the housing manager not less than four weeks' written notice expiring on any Monday or by the council giving similar notice to the tenant'. The council served a notice to quit on Mr D at the premises.

The Court of Appeal held that this service was not sufficient to determine the tenancy as it was not personal service and the council could not prove that the notice came to Mr D's attention. The council could not rely on section 196 of LPA 1925 as the service of

the notice was not required by the tenancy agreement as the standard term was not incorporated. The court indicated that it was likely the term would have been sufficient to 'require' the service of a notice to quit for the purposes of section 196 had it been incorporated.
Enfield LBC v Devonish and Sutton (1996)

Termination of licences

Secure licences

These can be brought to an end in the same way as secure tenancies. It is therefore necessary to have grounds for possession, to serve a notice seeking possession and to obtain a court order.

Non-secure licences

In general terms a licence is terminated by the landlord giving the licensee notice that it wishes to end the licence. Where the licence is contractual, housing officers should check the contract for a provision for what length of notice must be given to terminate it. Where such provision exists, this is the length of notice that should be given, subject to the following exceptions.

First, where the licence is protected by PEA 1977, the minimum notice period is 28 days. Therefore, the contractual notice period must be ignored if it is less than 28 days. The notice must be in writing and contain the prescribed information specified by PEA 1977 (most social landlords have standard forms which contain the prescribed information). Any specific requirements in the contract of how the notice should be given must also be followed.

Secondly, where the licence is an excluded licence *and* no provision is made in the contract for notice, it can be ended by the licensor giving reasonable notice. What amounts to reasonable notice depends on the facts. A long-term occupier may require more than 28 days' notice.

The most common circumstances where only reasonable notice is required are where the licence:

- is a bare licence (see p. 54 above);
- was granted as a temporary expedient to persons who entered the land as trespassers (see p. 55 above);
- is of hostel accommodation owned by a local authority.

Trespassers

Trespassers have no right to be on land. As long as the landlord has terminated any previous tenancy or licence it is entitled to immediate possession. Accordingly, no notice is required before bringing proceedings to evict trespassers. Many social landlords do, however, serve a precautionary notice terminating any interest that may have been granted to guard against later claims by the occupiers that they were granted a licence which has not been properly terminated.

Checklist for terminating rights of occupation

Tenancy

- Secure tenancy: Need grounds, serve section 83 notice, get court order
- Assured tenancy: Need grounds, serve section 8 notice, get court order
- Assured shorthold: Serve section 21 notice, get court order
- Non-secure tenancy:
  - —Protected by PEA: Serve notice to quit, minimum notice 28 days, get court order
  - —Excluded tenancy: Serve notice to quit, no requirement for court order

Licence

- Secure licence: Need grounds, serve section 83 notice, get court order
- Contractual licence:
  —Protected by PEA: Give notice according to contract, subject to 28 days minimum, get court order
  —Excluded: Give notice according to contract or, if none specified, reasonable notice, no need for court order
- Bare licence: Give reasonable notice, no need for court order

Part III

Common Management Problems

8.
Common Management Problems

Tenant leaving property / Tenant wishing to give up tenancy / Death of the tenant

Housing managers need to be able to deal with many kinds of recurrent problem. Dealing with housing management problems properly in the first instance usually avoids litigation, but where litigation does arise a good understanding of the legal issues involved as well as the issues relevant to the case ensures that managers do not waste valuable public resources on doomed court proceedings. This chapter explores the three main problems which occur regularly, namely the tenant leaving the property, the tenant wishing to give up the property, and the tenant's death, with particular regard to granting transfer of occupation rights and to acquisition and loss of statutory protection.

Tenant leaving property

There are three main situations detailed below where the tenant leaves the property, and where housing managers need to decide whether to take action.

Management transfer

Commonly, the tenant leaves the property because of a management transfer to other accommodation owned by the social landlord. This in itself does not determine the tenancy of the first property, although it does mean that the tenancy ceases to be secure (see further A. Dymond, *Security of Tenure* (2nd edn, Arden's Housing Library, 2000), p. 43). It is therefore necessary to end the tenancy by serving a notice to quit (see pp. 73–77 above). As a matter of good practice the housing officer should serve the tenant with such notice in relation to the first property when the tenant is allowed into occupation of the new property. Thus the landlord can deal with the property as it wishes and avoid any problems which may arise in serving the tenant personally if he or she later leaves the second property without informing the landlord.

Abandonment

Here, the tenant leaves the property for a long period and the housing officer later discovers that the property is empty or that there are other people in occupation. If the tenant has abandoned the property, the tenancy ceases to be secure. However, the tenant's absence only indicates that the tenancy is no longer secure if it can be shown that he or she has ceased to occupy the premises as his or her only or principal home.

It is useful to think of this requirement in two parts: (a) is the tenant still in occupation of the premises at all? (b) if so, is the tenant occupying the premises as his or her only or principal home?

A tenant is in occupation of the premises, despite not being physically present, if he or she intends to return to them *and* has left some physical signs of occupation in them. These signs can range from leaving significant belongings there to leaving someone else in occupation to act as a caretaker. It is clearly difficult for a housing manager to show whether the tenant intends to return and, after a sufficiently long absence, it is for the tenant to prove that he or she is still in occupation. If there are letters on the housing file from the tenant or notes of conversations which appear to demonstrate that he or she does intend to return, it is obvious that the tenant can show the required intention. Even if the timescale is lengthy, this does not prevent the tenant from occupying the premises provided there are some physical signs of occupation.

If it is concluded that the tenant is in occupation, the question becomes whether the premises are his or her only or principal home. Ultimately it is a matter of fact and degree in any particular case. Factors that might point away from this issue include some or all of the following:

- the tenant has another home elsewhere;
- the tenant lives there with his or her family;
- the tenant's children go to school there; and
- the tenant plans to stay there for a long time.

Where a tenant is forced to move around a lot because of his or her job, it is likely that the tenant's main base is the only or principal home, even if the tenant cannot spend much time there.

Case reports

In 1985, Mr Sawyer left premises, which he held on a council tenancy, to live with his girlfriend. The gas and electricity were cut off, although he continued to pay rent and rates. He visited the premises about once a month and, on one occasion, spent a week there. In 1986, Mr Sawyer told the council's representative that he and his girlfriend were purchasing her house together. The council served notice to quit on 29 August 1986, expiring on 30 September. By that time Mr Sawyer and his girlfriend had broken up, but he had not yet moved back. He gave evidence that he had had every intention of returning to the premises. The judge in the county court held that Mr Sawyer had at all times occupied the premises as his only or principal home. The Court of Appeal did not interfere with this finding. *Crawley BC v Sawyer* (1987)

Mr Swann, a secure tenant of council premises, bought a new property. He registered with British Telecom as a residential customer from that address, wrote a certain amount of correspondence from there, gave that address as his residence in letters to the Metropolitan Police and changed his firearms certificate to that address. The county court judge held that he had ceased to occupy the premises of which he had a tenancy as his only or principal home, which was affirmed by the Court of Appeal. *Sutton LBC v Swann* (1985)

Mr Ansah was an assured tenant of a flat in a house owned by the Ujima Housing Association. One of the other tenants in the house started to cause a nuisance and to harass him and his family. As a result, he decided to sublet the flat and took his family to live with his cousin and her family in a house which was being bought on a mortgage, to which he was a party. He let the flat furnished, but took all his other personal belongings with him. He always intended to return to the flat and had always regarded it as his only or principal home. In January 1996, he gave the subtenant notice that he required possession of the flat. On 4 June 1996, however, the housing association served notice to quit on Mr Ansah and the subtenant, and commenced possession proceedings on 2 August. On 29 August, Mr Ansah returned to live in the property.

In the county court, the judge held that the tenancy was still assured because Mr Ansah occupied the premises as his only or principal home. The Court of Appeal allowed the association's appeal and held that, as Mr Ansah was no longer in occupation of the flat, the burden was on him to show that he was still occupying the flat as his only or principal home, on the basis of an objective assessment of his actions and intention. Simply leaving his furniture there was not sufficient as this was consistent with a furnished letting. Further, he had granted an immediate right of occupation of the property to other people and was unable to resume occupation unless they gave up possession or he obtained a court order. Thus, he had not shown that he was occupying the premises as his only or principal home when the notice to quit expired and the housing association was entitled to possession. *Ujima Housing Association v Ansah* (1997)

Absence through holidays, even if such absence is for lengthy periods (e.g. to visit family abroad), does not in itself jeopardise occupation as the only or principal home. Additionally, a tenant may lose his or her security by ceasing to occupy premises as his or her only or principal home, but may regain it by returning to reoccupy them.

There are several possible explanations why the tenant does not occupy the premises and others occupy them instead. The current occupants may simply be caretaking the premises in the tenant's absence, may be squatters who have moved into abandoned premises, or may be subletting the property from the tenant. The housing officer must gather as much information about the circumstances as possible. The occupiers should be asked how they came to occupy the property (e.g. are they agents of the tenant, or are they paying rent on their own behalf?), of the tenant's whereabouts, whether there is a contact address or telephone number and the reasons for the tenant's absence. Where the officer suspects that they do not know the tenant, he or she can ask questions about the tenant, such as the number and age of their children, to establish whether it is likely that the occupiers are who they say they are. Neighbours can be approached for evidence as they may know where the tenant is or whether he or she has been at the premises. Any leads to the tenant's whereabouts should be followed up and the tenant should be asked to explain the situation. The most effective evidence in cases of this sort is an admission from the tenant that he or she no longer lives in the premises.

Further possible avenues to explore include housing benefit, council tax or income support records. If the tenant is claiming these benefits from other premises, this points towards those other premises being the only or principal home. It can also prove fruitful to hire enquiry agents who may be able to collect further evidence of where the tenant really lives.

If the housing officer concludes that the tenant has abandoned the property, the tenancy can be ended by the proper service of a notice to quit (see pp. 73–77 above). If a tenant returns to the property before the notice to quit expires, he or she may regain security and the notice is ineffective to terminate the tenancy (*Hussey v Camden LBC* (1994)). It is therefore advisable, where a notice to quit is served, for the housing officer to attend the premises on the day the notice to quit expires to confirm that the tenant has not returned. Unauthorised occupiers will try to argue that the service of the notice is inadequate to terminate the tenancy. Housing officers therefore need to be careful to ensure that service is sufficient.

Matrimonial property and cohabitees

Occupation by the tenant's spouse is deemed to be occupation by the tenant where the property is or was the matrimonial home (Family Law Act (FLA) 1996, s. 30). Rent paid by the non-tenant spouse must be accepted by the landlord to satisfy the tenant's liability. Further, a tenant does not lose his or her security of tenure if absent from the property as long as the non-tenant spouse occupies it as his or her only or principal home. This situation subsists for so long as the parties remain married, even if, for example, the tenant is granted another secure or assured tenancy.

Where the parties have divorced or have been cohabiting, the non-tenant partner (or ex-partner) may apply to the court for an order giving rights of occupation of

1. in the case of former spouses, the matrimonial home or any property intended by them to be their matrimonial home (FLA 1996, s. 35); and
2. in the case of cohabitants or former cohabitants, any property in which they have lived or intended to live together as husband and wife (FLA 1996, s. 36).

Such an order lasts, in the first instance, for up to six months, but can be extended for further six-month periods by the court. Once an order has been made, the non-tenant partner (or ex-partner) has the same rights to occupy the property as a non-tenant spouse (see above). Thus, the tenant does not lose his or her security of tenure for as long as the partner (or ex-partner) occupies the premises as his or her only or principal home.

There is no similar legal right for same sex partners.

Subletting

Secure tenants

All secure tenants have the right to take in lodgers. They may not sublet any part of the dwelling-house without the landlord's written consent. If the tenant sublets the whole of the premises, he or she immediately loses his or her security for good (HA 1985, s. 93(2)). This means that even if he or she moves back into the premises as his or her only or principal home, he or she is no longer a secure tenant. Where there are suspicions that a property is being sublet, the housing officer should try to gather as much evidence as possible. In some (rare) cases, there is a written tenancy agreement between the tenant and the occupiers and a copy should be obtained. Sometimes occupiers will admit to paying money to the tenant for their occupation. In those circumstances, the officer should enquire whether the tenant ever comes back to stay in the premises, whether he or she keeps a room for his or her own use or whether the occupiers have full use of the property.

Assured tenants

The position is different for assured tenants. They can only sublet the whole or any part of the premises with the landlord's consent, although a subletting without such consent (known as an unlawful subtenancy) is still valid. The landlord can take possession proceedings for breach of a term of the tenancy (HA 1988, Sched. 2, ground 12). If they do sublet the whole, the premises usually cease to be their only or principal home. This is the case even if the premises are sublet on an assured shorthold tenancy. Whether the tenant loses his or her security depends on whether, objectively, it appears that the tenant intended to return (*Ujima Housing Association v Ansah* (1997)—see p. 86 above). Where the tenant sublets with the landlord's consent and the landlord brings the head tenancy to an end, it is bound by the subtenancy; the subtenant becomes the landlord's direct tenant (HA 1988, s. 18).

Tenant wishing to give up tenancy

Tenants who wish to give up their tenancies may attempt it in three main ways: by serving a notice to quit, by surrendering the tenancy, or by assigning the tenancy to someone else. Tenants often try to do this in informal ways, which may not satisfy the legal requirements. It is important for housing officers to understand the legal requirements of these methods for two reasons.

1. They are then in a better position to help the tenant validly to give up the tenancy.
2. It enables them to know whether in any particular case the tenant has given up the tenancy. This means that they know whether the landlord is immediately entitled to possession of the premises or whether the occupiers have acquired any rights to be there.

Tenant's notice to quit

The tenant can give notice to quit in exactly the same way as the landlord (see pp. 74–77 above). One of two joint tenants can serve a notice to quit; this is sufficient to determine the tenancy. The periods of notice and the expiry date are the same as for a landlord's notice and the notice must be in writing. There is no prescribed information, however, to be included in a tenant's notice. The notice period runs from the date on which the landlord is served. If the notice period is insufficient, the landlord and tenant can agree to treat the notice as sufficient notice. However, if the notice is served by one of two or more joint tenants, such agreement has to be made by all parties. Where a tenant serves a notice to quit because of domestic violence, it is very unlikely that the joint tenant will agree to treat it as valid. The only solution in that case is to ask the tenant who has left to serve a further, valid, notice, but he or she will often be unwilling to do so.

Social landlords often provide standard notice to quit forms for tenants to fill in. These should make it clear on their face that the consequence of the notice is that the tenancy will come to an end. There should be guidance about the date on which the notice is to expire (e.g. that the notice is to expire on a Monday, if the rent is payable on Mondays). There is also a form of words which can be used so that the notice is valid even if the tenant makes a mistake: after the space for the expiry date of the notice should be the words 'or on the expiry of a complete period of the tenancy not less than 28 days from the date of service of this notice'.

Surrender

A surrender is an agreement between the landlord and tenant that the tenant will give up the tenancy and therefore cease to be liable for the rent. A surrender either can be express or can arise by operation of law.

An express surrender is unusual with residential tenancies; it has to be made by deed (which is a formal signed agreement which states that it is a deed, which is witnessed and usually sealed).

A surrender by operation of law occurs where the tenant does something inconsistent with the tenancy's continued existence and when the landlord then by its conduct accepts that the tenancy has ended. For example, if the tenant tells the landlord he or she is moving away and wants to end the tenancy and hands over the keys, and the landlord closes the rent account and prepares to relet the property, there is a surrender by operation of law.

The tenant's conduct must be enough to demonstrate that he or she is treating the tenancy as at an end. It is not enough to show that the tenant left the property owing rent. However, if the tenant leaves the property owing a very substantial sum of money and is absent for a substantial time, this may well be sufficient to found an argument that there has been a surrender.

It is not sufficient that there is action by the tenant alone. There must also be conduct on the landlord's part which demonstrates that it has accepted the surrender. Closing the rent account is such conduct. Conversely, any demand by the landlord for rent completely negates any argument that there has been a surrender. The service of a notice to quit, although tending to suggest that the landlord considers the tenancy is still in existence, is not necessarily inconsistent with a surrender by operation of law. Therefore, where a notice is served and it turns out that the notice itself or the service was invalid, it may be possible to argue that there has been a surrender.

Housing managers must be cautious in one aspect of surrender: if the tenant has sublet the premises, with or without permission, and the landlord accepts the surrender, it is bound by those tenancies. The subtenants, who are possibly unlawful, become tenants directly from the landlord and then acquire security of tenure. Therefore, before doing anything which could amount to acceptance of surrender, the officer should visit the premises to see if they are occupied by someone other than the tenant. If so, the officer should attempt to find out whether the occupiers are paying rent to the tenant. If they are, the rent account should be kept open and the landlord must recover possession by other means.

Case reports

The defendants, Mr Sharma and Ms Vyas, were in a relationship together and had two children. Mr Sharma also had two children from a previous relationship. He had a tenancy of a flat owned by Brent LBC, where they lived together. He moved out, surrendering the tenancy, and Brent granted Ms Vyas a sole tenancy of the flat. Ms Vyas later moved to Milton Keynes where she was granted a tenancy, but Mr Sharma had returned and remained in the flat with his own two children. Ms Vyas wrote to Brent in November 1988 saying that she had moved out and that she had no objection to the tenancy being transferred to Mr Sharma. At that stage there were rent arrears of over £4,000. From 12 December 1988, Brent stopped debiting rent in respect of the tenancy and on 16 December 1988 served a notice to quit at the premises.

In the county court, the judge found that the notice to quit was ineffective as it had not been properly served but that there had been a surrender by operation of law. The Court of Appeal held that the court has to look at the whole of the landlord's conduct. It was quite plain that Ms Vyas was treating the tenancy as ended from her letter and that this was accepted by Brent, demonstrated by a combination of no longer charging rent and the service of a notice to quit in the knowledge that Ms Vyas was not in possession or occupation of the premises. The service of the notice was not, in the circumstances, inconsistent with Brent unequivocally showing that the tenancy no longer existed. *Brent LBC v Sharma & Vyas* (1992)

Miss Butler, the tenant of the plaintiff, lived in the premises with Mr Scalley until April 1990. In July 1990, the plaintiff discovered that Miss Butler was no longer living in the premises and refused to accept rent from Mr Scalley. The plaintiff served a precautionary notice to quit and tried to persuade Miss Butler to acknowledge that her tenancy had been surrendered or to surrender it. She refused to do so. The plaintiff took possession proceedings. At trial the evidence was that Miss Butler had left most of her possessions and her cats in the premises. She went in to feed the cats and throughout 1990 had been considering whether there should be a reconciliation with Mr Scalley. The county court judge was satisfied that Miss Butler wanted nothing more to do with the premises, inferred a surrender by operation of law and ordered possession. The Court of Appeal allowed Mr Scalley's appeal and held that the evidence before the judge did not amount to the unequivocal conduct required to draw an inference of surrender by operation of law. *Chamberlain v Scalley* (1992)

Islington LBC let a flat to Mr Zionmor on a secure tenancy in 1992. He claimed the right to buy, which was acknowledged by the council in October 1995. In November 1995, he left the flat, leaving a friend in occupation and a note on the notice board saying, 'To those that have written graffiti on the walls by my flat and have smashed my windows and interfered with my door locks please note I no longer reside at [the flat]'. The friend moved out and the council discovered the flat completely empty except for a wardrobe and with all the windows smashed. The council boarded up the windows, changed the locks and closed the rent account.

Mr Zionmor telephoned the following day and was told that the council had treated the flat as abandoned. In proceedings between Mr Zionmor and the council, the issue arose whether he had surrendered his tenancy. The Court of Appeal held that the facts did not support the inference that he had relinquished possession of the flat in November 1995: the act of leaving a friend in the flat was inconsistent with a relinquishment and the note on the noticeboard was not addressed to the council. It did not suggest that he was giving up possession in any technical or legal sense. One of the judges also suggested that boarding up the windows and securing the front door were not sufficiently unequivocal as to amount to an acceptance of the surrender, as they were acts consistent with the council's duty to safeguard its housing stock. *Zionmor v Islington LBC* (1997)

Mrs Toth was a secure tenant of Croydon LBC. In late 1983, her husband left her: he was wanted by the police for robbery. A few days later, four men appeared, alleging that he owed them money and saying that if she did not get it, they would harm her and her baby. She left the premises, taking what belongings she could and storing the rest in her garage. She eventually applied to the council as homeless and was housed temporarily pending inquiries. In the meantime, the council had been informed that the premises had been abandoned. It changed the locks and relet the premises.

The council decided that Mrs Toth was intentionally homeless and sought possession of the temporary accommodation. Her solicitors then stated that she had never intended to give up her tenancy, but had moved out temporarily because of the harassment. The court held that she had surrendered

> her tenancy. She had given up possession and the council had taken possession by changing the locks and reletting. A subsequent assertion by the tenant that she had no intention of leaving permanently was not relevant as it was necessary to look at the situation when the council accepted the surrender. *R v Croydon LBC, ex p Toth* (1987)

Assignment

An assignment is an agreement between the tenant and a third party whereby the tenant transfers his or her interest in the property to the third party. The tenant is the 'assignor' and the third party the 'assignee'. If all the tenant has done is to sell the occupiers the key, no assignment has taken place.

Secure tenancies

In the case of a secure tenancy, an assignment is not possible except in limited circumstances:

- by way of mutual exchange;
- pursuant to a property adjustment order made in matrimonial proceedings or an order for financial relief in proceedings concerning children; and
- to a person who would be qualified to succeed the tenant if the tenant died immediately before the assignment.

A person is qualified to succeed the tenant only if:

1. the tenant is not him- or herself a successor, and
2. the person occupies the premises as his or her only or principal home and is either
   (a) the tenant's spouse, or
   (b) another member of the tenant's family (which includes a person with whom the tenant lived as husband or wife, but not a partner in a same-sex relationship) who has resided with the tenant for the preceding twelve months.

Assured tenancies

In the case of an assured tenancy, there are no such restrictions on the person to whom a tenant can assign.

It is a term of every assured tenancy and of many secure tenancies that the tenant cannot assign without the landlord's consent. However, if the tenant does assign without consent, the assignment is still valid (*Peabody Donation Fund v Higgins* (1983)). The landlord is then required to take possession proceedings for breach of the tenancy agreement.

Formal requirements

If an assignment is not in writing, it is invalid and has no effect (Law of Property (Miscellaneous Provisions) Act 1989, s. 2). Therefore, when an occupier claims to have been granted an assignment, the housing officer should ask whether the assignment was oral or written. If it was oral, the officer can be sure that no valid assignment has taken place (but note the exception below). If it was written, the officer should ask for a copy. A written assignment may not be binding on the landlord unless it was by deed (*Crago v Julian* (1992); see also C. Hunter, *Tenants' Rights* (Arden's Housing Library, 1995), pp. 33–35). Where the assignment is not by deed but is in writing, it can take effect, but usually only as between the tenant and the third party. The landlord may be bound by the assignment if it can be said to have been a party to it (e.g. by accepting rent from the assignee, knowing of the assignment).

An oral assignment is effective if the landlord expressly or impliedly agrees to the assignee becoming the tenant and the assignee expressly or impliedly agrees to the new arrangement. The landlord is in fact taken to have granted a new tenancy, which can be done orally, and the old tenant's interest ends by surrender by operation of law.

Terms of tenancy

Where there is a proper assignment, the assignee is bound by those covenants in the tenancy agreement which can be said to touch and concern the land (e.g. payment of rent or repair). Where the assignment is not in writing and there is deemed to be a grant of a new tenancy, the landlord's standard conditions of tenancy are not incorporated into the tenancy unless there is express agreement that they should be. Housing officers need to ensure that such an agreement is recorded so that the covenants in the tenancy conditions can be enforced against the new tenant.

Death of the tenant

A tenancy is like any other property and can be inherited under the terms of a tenant's will. If the tenant dies intestate (without making a will), the tenancy is inherited according to the rules of intestacy. This general position has been modified by statute for secure and assured tenancies, as set out below. As a result, the tenant's death does not end the tenancy, but it can affect its security or whether the landlord can bring possession proceedings.

Assured tenancy

The consequences of the tenant's death depend on whether he or she was a sole tenant. If not, the tenancy simply remains in the other joint tenants. If he or she was a sole tenant and his or her spouse was living in the premises as his or her only or principal home immediately before the tenant's death, the tenancy vests automatically in the spouse unless the tenant was him- or herself a successor. Where there is no spouse or the tenant was a successor, the tenancy passes in accordance with his or her will or intestacy.

Where the tenancy was periodic and has not vested in the tenant's spouse but has devolved under his or her will or intestacy, the landlord can apply for possession under mandatory ground 7 of Schedule 2 to HA 1988 as long as proceedings are begun within 12 months of either the former tenant's death or the date on which the landlord became aware of the death.

Secure tenancy

Succession to a secure tenancy is governed by whether there is anyone entitled to succeed to it under section 87 of HA 1985. This is only the case if the tenant was not him- or herself a successor. Where the tenant was not a successor, the following people are qualified to succeed to the tenancy if they occupied the premises as their only or principal home when the tenant died:

1. the tenant's spouse; or
2. a member of the tenant's family (including a person who lived with the tenant as husband and wife, but not a same-sex partner) who had resided with him or her during the 12 months prior to his or her death.

Where there is no-one entitled to succeed to a secure tenancy, it ceases to be secure. However, the contractual tenancy still exists and passes in accordance with the provisions of the will or intestacy. The tenancy can be determined by notice to quit. The person on whom the notice should be served depends on whether the tenant made a will or died intestate. It is therefore necessary to make inquiries with the next of kin about whether the tenant made a will. If he or she did, the executors' names and addresses should be discovered. Usually the executors of any will would contact the local authority to address the disposal of the tenancy.

Where the tenant made a will, the notice to quit should name and be served personally on the executors. (If section 196 of LPA 1925 applies to the tenancy it is sufficient to serve the notice at the property.) If there are no executors or the tenant did not make a will, the notice to quit should be addressed to the tenant's personal representatives and served on them at the tenant's last known residential or business address (in most cases this will be at the property); a copy of the notice, similarly addressed, must also be served on the Public Trustee. Once personal representatives are appointed, the notice should name and be served on them. If the local authority cannot find out the names of the personal representatives from the tenant's relatives, it can lodge an application for a standing search at the Probate Registry. The Registry will send out an office copy entry of any grant issued not more than 12 months before nor more than six months after the date of the application. Similarly, the notice should be served personally on the personal representatives unless the provisions of section 196 of LPA 1925 apply.

Where housing officers consider that there is no-one qualified to succeed to the tenancy, they should be aware that someone may later come forward claiming to succeed to the property. Where this claim is disputed by the local authority, court proceedings to establish the claim usually follow. If the occupier is successful, he or she is deemed to be the secure tenant of the property from the date of the previous tenant's death. This commonly results in under-occupation of the property, which in turn can bring about a ground for possession under ground 16 of Schedule 2 to HA 1985. To rely on this ground, however, a notice seeking possession must have been served on the tenant between six and twelve months after the previous tenant's death. It is therefore advisable, where it appears that a claim may be made to a succession which would result in under-occupation, to serve a precautionary notice under ground 16, in addition to and stated to be 'without prejudice' to the operation of any notice to quit.

Examples

Management transfer

Miss Vincent was an assured tenant of the Victoria Housing Association at 11 Francis Gardens. The tenancy had no provision for service of notices and section 196 of the LPA 1925 did not apply. The property fell into disrepair and, as a result, the housing association agreed to transfer the tenant and give her a tenancy of 17 Francis Gardens. Number 11 was boarded up and remained so for many years. Miss Vincent then moved away and the association did not have her address. Squatters moved into number 11 and the housing association wants to evict them. Miss Vincent's tenancy has not been brought to an end and she cannot be traced to serve a notice to quit. While it may be possible to argue that she surrendered her tenancy to number 11, the housing association would be in a much better position if it had

(a) served her with a notice to quit number 11 when she moved into number 17; or
(b) asked her to surrender her tenancy of number 11 by deed.

Abandonment

Mr Little was a secure tenant of Norchester District Council. In 1993, he was convicted of burglary and sentenced to five years in prison. He arranged for his brother to live in his property to look after it and pay the rent while he was in prison. He wrote to the housing office saying that he intended to come back to the property after serving his sentence. The council wanted to bring possession proceedings. It was, however, not able to do so. None of the grounds for possession of a secure tenancy was satisfied and Mr Little had not ceased to occupy the premises as his only or principal home: he was still in occupation through his brother, his possessions and his intention to return to the premises when he came out and he had no other home. By 1995, Mr Little's brother decided to move out and he took all Mr Little's belongings with him. The council was then able to serve a notice to quit because Mr Little had lost his security: there was no physical sign of occupation, so, despite his intention to return to the property, he was no longer occupying it.

Tenant's notice to quit

Mr and Mrs Large had a joint tenancy from the Norchester District Council of 1 Riverside. Their marriage started to break down and Mr Large used to beat Mrs Large. She applied for help from the council, and was given temporary accommodation in a hostel. She was told that she would be rehoused, but that she had to serve notice to quit to bring the joint tenancy to an end. On 1 October, she picked up one of the council's standard form notices and took it back to the hostel to complete. She filled in the date of expiry of the notice as 3 November, which was a rent day and more than 28 days from the date she filled in the form. She did not take the notice into the housing office, however, until 10 October, which was only 24 days from the date of expiry. The notice did not contain any saving clause. The council did not check the dates and rehoused her. Possession proceedings were started against Mr Large, but had to be withdrawn because the notice to quit was not valid. It had to be *served*, and not simply filled in, at least 28 days from the date of expiry. The invalidity could not be waived by Mrs Large alone because it was a joint tenancy.

Assignment and matrimonial property
Miss Warwick was the tenant of the Victoria Housing Association. Her partner, Mr Belgrave, moved in with her and they had two children together. After five years, Miss Warwick left Mr Belgrave and the children. Before she left, she told Mr Belgrave that he could have the tenancy. He informed the housing office. The housing association, however, told him that they were not willing for him to be the tenant and that any rent was accepted only on behalf of Miss Warwick. Miss Warwick had not assigned her tenancy to Mr Belgrave because the 'assignment' was not in writing and her wishes did not bind the housing association. The housing association then told Mr Belgrave that Miss Warwick had lost her security of tenure and that it would serve a notice to quit. Mr Belgrave immediately took advice and applied to the court and obtained an order under section 36 of FLA 1996, giving him rights of occupation of the property. The housing association was then unable to serve a notice to quit as his occupation was deemed to be that of Miss Warwick, who was therefore occupying the premises as her only or principal home and regained her security of tenure.

Death of tenant
Mrs Jones was the tenant of the Norchester District Council. She had a three-bedroomed property. During the last year of her life, her grandson came to live with her. When she died, he claimed to succeed to the

tenancy. The council disputed his right to succeed as it did not consider that he had lived in the property for 12 months before Mrs Jones died. The grandson applied to the court for a declaration that he was the tenant. The court was satisfied that he had lived there for 12 months before her death and granted the declaration. By that time, it was 15 months after Mrs Jones' death. The council was therefore unable to serve a notice seeking possession under ground 16 for under-occupation and lost the use of a three-bedroomed property. The housing officer should have served a 'without prejudice' notice seeking possession between 6 and 12 months after Mrs Jones' death. The council would then have been able to give the grandson a one-bedroomed flat as suitable alternative accommodation and free up a three-bedroomed house.

Mr and Mrs Tachbrook were joint assured weekly tenants of the Victoria Housing Association. Mrs Tachbrook died and Mr Tachbrook became the sole tenant. He later remarried and left the tenancy to his second wife in his will. When he died, his second wife could not succeed to the tenancy under section 17 of HA 1988 because he was already a successor. Therefore the tenancy devolved on her under the will and the housing association was able to bring possession proceedings against her under ground 7 of Schedule 2 within 12 months of Mr Tachbrook's death.

Key points

Housing managers need to understand the legal problems which arise when a tenant leaves the property, wishes to give up the tenancy or dies.

Tenant leaves property

- Where a tenant is given a management transfer, when he or she takes up occupation of the new property, the housing officer should either serve a notice to quit the old property or ask the tenant to sign an agreement surrendering the old tenancy.

- When a tenant is absent from the property, there may be many explanations. The tenancy ceases to be secure if the tenant has abandoned the property or, in the case of a secure tenancy, sublet the whole of the property.
- Security can be regained if the tenant comes back to live in the property as his or her only or principal home except in the case of a secure tenant who has sublet the whole of the property.
- To establish if the tenant has lost security of tenure through absence, the housing manager must establish whether the tenant is still in occupation at all (which involves there being physical signs of occupation coupled with an intention to return) and whether it is the tenant's only or principal home. If the tenant is away for a long time, the onus is on him or her to establish that security has not been lost.
- Where the property is occupied by the tenant's spouse or partner or ex-partner with occupation rights under section 35 or 36 of FLA 1996, the tenancy remains secure or assured despite the tenant's absence.

Tenant wishes to give up tenancy

- A tenant can serve a notice to quit on the landlord to end the tenancy. It must comply with the formal requirements.
- In the case of a sole tenancy, the landlord and tenant can waive any defect in the notice. In the case of a joint tenancy, both the tenants must agree to any waiver. In practice, this means that a joint tenant's notice to quit must be valid to be effective.
- A tenant can surrender the tenancy either expressly or by operation of law.
- An express surrender must be by deed.
- A surrender by operation of law requires the tenant and the landlord to act unequivocally in a way that is inconsistent with the continuation of the tenancy.

- If the landlord accepts a surrender, any subtenants, whether lawful or not, become tenants directly of the landlord.
- A tenant may try to assign the tenancy. There are restrictions on when secure tenancies can be assigned. In general, it is a breach of the tenancy agreement to assign an assured tenancy without the landlord's consent.
- To be valid at law, an assignment must be by deed. An assignment which is in writing is usually valid between the assignor and assignee but does not bind the landlord unless the landlord acts so as to be a party to it. An oral assignment has no effect, although a landlord must ensure that it does not create a new tenancy by accepting the assignee as a tenant.

Death of tenant

- When the tenant dies, the tenancy does not come to an end. There are statutory provisions for what happens to it.
- Secure tenancies vest in a person qualified to succeed to the tenancy. If there is no person qualified to succeed, the tenancy becomes non-secure and can be determined by a notice to quit.
- In the case of assured tenancies, a spouse can succeed to the tenancy under the statute. Otherwise, the tenancy passes under the tenant's will or intestacy. If it does so, there is a mandatory ground for possession.
- In either case, there can only be one statutory succession.

Part IV

Possession Proceedings

9.
Choosing the Type of Proceedings

In most cases where premises are occupied without the landlord's consent, it will be necessary to go to court to obtain an order for possession. Taking direct physical action to repossess premises (such as changing the locks) is only lawful against occupiers who came onto the land as trespassers and those who are excluded from statutory protection (see Chap. 6). Direct physical repossession of premises can be risky (see pp. 140–141 below). First, there is the danger of committing an offence under section 6 of the Criminal Law Act 1977 if the occupiers are present on the premises. Secondly, there is the risk that the occupiers may later establish that they had been given a tenancy or a licence of the property. In those circumstances, civil proceedings for unlawful eviction may follow, or even prosecution under section 1 of PEA 1977. In most cases, therefore, the safest course is to bring court proceedings.

Before bringing proceedings, the landlord must ensure that it has an immediate right to possession of the premises. This entails finding out who is currently occupying the premises and what right, if any, they have to be there. Any rights of occupation granted by the landlord (such as a previous tenancy or any licence) must also be ended. Such rights may be held not by the occupiers themselves, but by a former tenant. Once the landlord has an immediate right to possession, it must decide which kind of possession proceedings are appropriate. There are four different types of proceedings:

- summary proceedings under CPR Schedule 2, CCR Order 24 Part I or Schedule 1, RSC Order 113;
- interim possession orders under CPR Schedule 2, CCR Order 24 Part II;
- injunctive proceedings; and
- ordinary possession proceedings.

Summary proceedings are quick proceedings which can be used when the occupiers are not tenants or former tenants of the landlord. They were designed for use particularly where the landlord does not know the occupiers' names. They are usually used against squatters.

Where the need for possession is even more urgent, an interim possession order can be sought. Interim possession proceedings are brought within the context of summary proceedings and provide a means by which the court can order possession before it has heard the summary proceedings. They must be brought within 28 days of the date on which the landlord first knew of the occupation of its property. They can only be brought against people who have at all times been trespassers on the property. Interim possession orders are enforced by the police and have criminal sanctions attached.

Injunction proceedings are unusual in this context, but are most commonly brought either where the landlord is not totally dispossessed or against known trespassers in cases of real urgency.

Ordinary possession proceedings can be brought against any known individual. They are the correct proceedings to use if the case is not completely straightforward or if the occupier is a tenant or former tenant of the landlord. They should also be used if the landlord wishes to seek damages and/or rent arrears. They are not as quick as the other kinds of proceedings.

Each of these types of proceedings is considered in further detail in the following chapters.

Example

The Victoria Housing Association owns a block of six flats called Emery Towers.

Flat 1: The last tenant of the flat was Mr Appleby. He has been rehoused after a management transfer and his tenancy of Flat 1 has been terminated. Pending repairs to the flat, some students have gained access to the property and are still living there despite having been asked to leave.

Flat 2: The occupant of Flat 2 is Mr Bessborough. He was being temporarily housed in the flat pursuant to a licence agreement while repairs were being done to the house of which he has a tenancy at 12 Frances Place. Now that repairs to 12 Frances Place are completed, he is refusing to leave Flat 2.

Flat 3: The last tenant of this flat was Mr Cresswell. In 1995, his brother and family came to stay and have never left. In October 1996, however, Mr Cresswell decided to move to Skegness and agreed to surrender his tenancy. The housing association closed his rent account in November 1996.

Flat 4: This flat is let to Miss Dawes. Three years ago she left the country, leaving her best friend in occupation of the flat. No action has been taken by her or by the housing association in the meantime.

Flat 5: Mr Ellwood, in breach of his tenancy agreement, has rented out this flat to some friends. The housing association has discovered that Mr Ellwood is living at 17 Morpeth Drive. The housing officer served him personally with a notice to quit which has now expired.

Flat 6: Mr Field, also in breach of his tenancy agreement, rented this flat to some people he met in the pub and went to live with his girlfriend. The people did not pay their rent and so six months later he wrote to the housing association asking to surrender the tenancy and enclosing his set of keys. The housing association agreed to the surrender and closed the rent account.

The housing association now want to get possession of all the flats in the block. In the case of flats 1, 2, 3 and 5, it can bring summary proceedings.

In the case of flat 4, the tenancy has not been determined, so proceedings cannot yet be brought. The housing association has to end Miss Dawes's tenancy by service of a notice to quit, and bring ordinary proceedings against her and the occupier.

In the case of Flat 6, the surrender by Mr Field operated to transfer his interest back to the housing association, subject to the subtenancies he had created, even though they were unlawful and the housing association had no notice of them at the date of the surrender. The illegal subtenants therefore became tenants holding directly from the housing association. The housing association can bring proceedings against the new tenants on ground 12 of Schedule 2 to HA 1988 for breach of the covenant against subletting. The court may not, however, consider it reasonable to grant possession.

10.
Summary Proceedings

When summary proceedings are available / When summary proceedings are appropriate / Procedure / Procedure at the hearing / Advantages and disadvantages

Summary possession proceedings were introduced in the early 1970s to provide a swift procedure that could be used against unauthorised occupiers whose identities were unknown. Previously, if the occupiers refused to give their names, a landowner had difficulty regaining possession. In the county court, proceedings are governed by CPR Schedule 2, CCR Order 24 Part I, and in the High Court by CPR Schedule 1, RSC Order 113.

When summary proceedings are available

Summary proceedings are not available where any occupier is either a tenant or a person whose tenancy has ended but who remains in occupation of the property. Summary proceedings *are* available, however, against occupiers who:

- entered the property as trespassers;
- entered the property with the consent of the person claiming possession, but who refuse to leave once that consent is revoked (i.e. former licensees);
- entered the property with the consent of a former tenant whose tenancy has ended and who has vacated the property;

- were illegal subtenants of a former tenant whose own tenancy has ended (other than by surrender) and who has vacated the property.

When summary proceedings are appropriate

Summary possession proceedings are designed to be quick. Evidence is given on affidavit, or by witness statement; it is not usual for oral evidence to be presented. A landlord is entitled to use summary proceedings if it can demonstrate that the case falls within one of the categories set out above. However, the case must be clear and straightforward (e.g. a case against squatters). If it is not, the court will not be convinced that the case is one where summary proceedings are available and will send the case to be tried in the normal way.

Summary proceedings can be brought where there is a disputed issue between the parties, but only where the applicant's affidavit or witness statement shows that the matter is clear and straightforward. It will often be the case, however, that what starts out as an open and shut case from the landlord's viewpoint becomes more complicated because of something raised by the occupier, which the landlord could not have foreseen. This, in itself, does not prevent the matter proceeding using summary proceedings where, in the judge's opinion, it is a matter which can be decided without requiring a full hearing to establish the facts. Similarly, where the only question is of the meaning of a written agreement, rather than the circumstances in which the agreement was made, then it is appropriate to use summary proceedings.

Where the disputed issue is more complicated and likely to involve disputed evidence, summary proceedings are not appropriate. For example, where the occupant is claiming to have succeeded to the previous tenancy and the landlord disputes that he or she is qualified to do so, the judge will need to hear witnesses to establish whose case is correct; ordinary possession proceedings should therefore be brought.

Examples of suitability

The following have been held not to be suitable for summary procedure:

1. Complicated questions of title of the person claiming possession.
2. Questions over whether an agreement which on its face was a licence was a sham, so that the occupiers were in fact tenants.
3. Questions over whether there had been a surrender of a tenancy by operation of law where the facts relied on by the landlord in his affidavit were not conclusive.

The following have been held to be suitable for summary procedure:

4. Questions over whether there had been a surrender of a tenancy by operation of law where the tenant had agreed to leave the property and had made representations to the landlord that he had in fact left it. This pointed unequivocally to his having surrendered the tenancy even though, at the hearing of the proceedings, he or she claimed that he or she had not left.

Procedure

Commencing proceedings

Summary proceedings can be brought in both the High Court and the county court. The jurisdiction of the county court is unlimited for summary proceedings; proceedings in the High Court are limited, however, to cases where the occupier is not protected by PEA 1977 (see Chap. 6). Landlords sometimes choose to bring proceedings in the High Court because they think that the case will be heard more quickly. This can lead to higher costs because where proceedings are commenced in the High Court which should have been commenced in the county court, the High Court has power to penalise the parties in costs. This chapter therefore deals primarily with proceedings in the county court.

The person or body claiming possession is known as the applicant and the occupiers are known as the respondents. Summary proceedings are commenced in the county court by a claim form, which sets out very briefly what the applicant is asking the court to do, that the applicant is entitled to possession and that the respondents are in occupation of the premises without the applicant's consent. If any of the occupiers' names are known they should be set out in the claim form, usually precedent form N312, but note that this form is not mandatory.

In support of the claim, the applicant must file an affidavit or witness statement stating:

- its interest in the land;
- the circumstances in which the land has been occupied without its licence or consent and the circumstances in which its claim to possession arises; and
- that it does not know the name of any person occupying the land who is not named in the originating summons.

This affidavit or witness statement is usually sworn or signed by the housing officer for the property. It forms the evidence on which the court will decide whether to give an order for possession. It is therefore important that it is as detailed as possible and contains everything necessary to prove the applicant's entitlement to possession. The preparation of affidavits and witness statements is discussed further in Chapter 15.

The court fixes a date (the 'return date') on which the claim for possession is to be heard.

Service

The claim form, affidavit or witness statement in support and a notice of the return date must be served on the occupiers of the property. This can be effected by an officer of the court or by the applicant.

The method of service to be used depends on whether any of the respondents' names are known. If some are known and some unknown, they must be served separately, as follows.

Service on named respondents

Known respondents must be served individually with the claim form, affidavit or witness statement and notice of the return date. If service is being carried out by the applicant, there are three possible ways.

1. The applicant may deliver the documents personally to the respondent. This means that the documents are to be left with the respondent. It is not enough simply to put the documents through the letterbox. It must be possible to show that the respondent received the documents, which usually requires physically handing him or her the documents. If the respondent refuses to take them, it is sufficient to inform him or her what the documents are and to throw them down in his or her presence. Handing over the documents in an envelope without telling him or her what they are, however, is not sufficient.
2. The applicant may serve the documents on the respondent's solicitor if the solicitor has notified the applicant that he or she is authorised to accept service on the respondent's behalf.
3. The court may provide for any other method of service.

Note that if the documents are served by the court, they can simply be served by post.

Service on unnamed respondents

Service on unknown respondents must be carried out in one of the following two ways:

1. A copy of each of the claim form, affidavit or witness statement and notice of the return day must be fixed to

the main door or other conspicuous part of the premises and a further copy of the documents must be put in a transparent, sealed envelope, addressed to the occupiers and put through the letterbox if there is one.

2. Stakes can be placed in the ground at conspicuous parts of the occupied property and copies of the documents must again be put into sealed transparent envelopes addressed to the occupiers and fixed to the stakes.

These methods are the same whether service is carried out by the applicant or by the court.

When service must be carried out

This is determined by reference to the return date. Where possession is being sought of residential premises, service must be not less than five clear days before the return date (i.e. there must be at least five whole days between the date of service and the return date). This means, for instance, that if the return date in the county court is on a Thursday, service must take place on or before the preceding Friday.

Where possession is being sought of non-residential land, there must be not less than two clear days between the date of service and the return date. These periods for service cannot include Saturday, Sunday, a bank holiday, Christmas Day or Good Friday, but can be shortened if the matter is one of urgency and the court allows it. This is dealt with on the return date.

Note that where documents are left at the premises, they are deemed to have been served on the *following* day.

Certificate of service

Where service has been carried out by the applicant, it must file a certificate of service within seven days of service of the claim form showing the date on which the documents were served and that the documents have not been returned undelivered.

Inadequate service

Irregularities in service may not be fatal to the proceedings. If all the occupiers attend the hearing and it can be shown that the proceedings came to the attention of all the occupiers in sufficient time, then proceedings may go ahead. Usually, however, proceedings are adjourned to allow proper service, resulting in unnecessary delay and expense.

Case report

Westminster City Council began summary proceedings against squatters. The claim form was put into an envelope addressed to 'Peter Chapman and persons unknown' and posted through the letterbox rather than fixed to the premises' main door as required by the County Court Rules. Peter Chapman was no longer in occupation of the house, but the other occupants opened the envelope and read the papers. They all attended the county court hearing in person and one objected to the validity of service. On appeal from the judge's decision that service had been effective, the Court of Appeal held that on the facts found by the judge, the method of service had been sufficient to bring the proceedings to the notice of all persons concerned more than seven days before the hearing. Therefore, although the rule had not been complied with, this was treated as an irregularity which had been cured on the facts. It would be otherwise if the applicant were unable to prove that the persons affected knew of the hearing before the minimum period of notice required by the rules. *Westminster City Council v Chapman and Persons Unknown* (1975)

Procedure at the hearing

Return date

If the matter is one of urgency, an early return date should be requested when the judge will decide whether the matter is sufficiently urgent for a shorter period of notice to be given.

If the judge finds it is not sufficiently urgent, the matter will be adjourned to allow sufficient time to elapse after service before the matter is actually heard. Despite the apparently short time limits in summary proceedings, it is common for weeks to elapse between proceedings being issued and the return date.

Appearance by unknown respondents

The return date is often the first time that any contact can be made with unknown occupiers. At the return date, they can request to be made parties to the proceedings and be joined as named respondents. This may result in the hearing being adjourned to give time for them to file an affidavit or witness statement setting out their case. An adjournment is not automatic, however, and the respondents must appear to have some form of defence to justify one being given.

The hearing

Summary procedure is designed to be quick, with evidence given in writing. The judge considers the affidavit or witness statement filed in support of the claim form, any certificate of service and any affidavit or witness statement filed or brought to court by the respondents. If no defence is raised, the judge decides the matter on the written evidence. If the respondents attend, they may request an adjournment to file written evidence (see above). The judge, however, may choose to hear oral evidence from the respondents and decide the matter there and then. This is only appropriate where the issues are clear and straightforward. If the judge is of the view that the respondents are raising a substantial defence, he or she may decide to adjourn the matter to allow the respondents to take legal advice and to serve evidence, and for the applicants to serve further evidence to rebut any defence raised.

It may be apparent, either at the first hearing or after the respondents have served their evidence, that the issues involved in deciding the case are more complex than originally anticipated. In those circumstances, the judge can order that the case should go to trial in the normal way and will give the appropriate directions.

It can also happen that a case which, at first sight, seemed appropriate for summary proceedings turns out to be a case to which summary procedure does not apply. An example of this could arise where a secure tenant apparently loses his or her security by leaving the premises, a notice to quit is served and summary proceedings are quite properly taken against the occupants of the premises whom the landlord believes to be trespassers. If the tenant then returns and wishes to argue that he or she had not lost security so that the service of a notice to quit did not terminate the tenancy, the proceedings would be against a tenant or a tenant holding over after the termination of the tenancy. Therefore, summary proceedings would not be available. The judge should be asked to give directions (e.g. for a defence to be filed) so that the matter can proceed to trial in the usual way.

The order for possession

If the judge is satisfied that the respondents have no right to be on the property, he or she will make a possession order. The order is usually in the form that the applicant do recover possession of the property forthwith (i.e. immediately). Where the respondents' entry onto the property was without consent in the first place, the judge has no power to suspend the order without the applicant's consent (see *McPhail v Persons Unknown* (1973)). In other cases, the court has the same powers to suspend the order as it would in ordinary possession proceedings (see Chap. 13).

It is not possible to get a money judgment in summary proceedings. If a landlord wishes to obtain damages for trespass, it must institute separate proceedings. Note that a costs order can only be made against a named respondent.

Warrant for possession

An application may be made for a warrant for possession at any time within a three-month period after the date specified for possession in the order. If more than three months elapse, it is necessary to go back to the court to obtain leave to issue the warrant.

A warrant for possession is effective against all occupiers of the property, whether or not they were parties to the original proceedings.

Advantages and disadvantages

The advantages of summary possession proceedings are:

- They are relatively quick—the whole process in practice taking about four to six weeks.
- They can be brought where the occupiers' identity is unknown.

The disadvantages are:

- They cannot be brought where it appears that possession is sought against a tenant or a tenant holding over after his or her tenancy has ended.
- There is no provision for a money claim under summary procedure.
- The case must be sufficiently clear and straightforward, otherwise it will be adjourned for a trial of the issues.

11. Interim Possession Proceedings

When interim possession orders are available / Procedure / Timetable for interim possession order / Advantages and disadvantages

Where summary proceedings are being used, but it is important to obtain possession before they can be heard, it is possible to apply for an interim possession order to be granted on a temporary basis pending the hearing of the main possession proceedings. It is available only in the county court under CPR Schedule 2, CCR Order 24 Part II. The respondents may only appear at the hearing if they have filed an affidavit or witness statement in the prescribed form. Interim possession orders are enforced by the police, not by a warrant for possession.

When interim possession orders are available

An application for an interim possession order can only be made if all the following conditions are satisfied:

- the only claim made is for possession of the whole or a self-contained part of a building or the land ancillary to it;
- the applicant has an immediate right to possession (i.e. there is no tenant through whom the occupiers could claim a right to possession) and has had such a right throughout the relevant period of unauthorised occupation;

- the unauthorised occupiers entered the premises without the applicant's consent (i.e. they are outright trespassers or squatters); and
- the claim has been brought within 28 days of the date on which the applicant first knew or ought to have known that any of the unauthorised occupiers were in occupation.

This procedure is available even if the occupiers' names are unknown.

Procedure

Commencing proceedings

All the documents required in an application for an interim possession order must be in the prescribed form. The applicant must file a claim form with a witness statement or affidavit in support (form N130) and an application notice (form N131). The affidavit or witness statement must be sworn by the applicant personally or, where the applicant is a body corporate such as a local authority or housing association, by an officer duly authorised to swear the affidavits or witness statement on its behalf. It is an offence knowingly or recklessly to make a false or misleading statement in an affidavit for the purpose of obtaining or resisting an interim possession order.

A time when the application will be considered is fixed by the court not less than three clear days after the application is issued.

Service

Service must be carried out by the applicant, not by the court. The applicant must serve the respondent with:

1. the application notice; and
2. a copy of the prescribed form for the respondent's affidavit or witness statement (form N133) within 24 hours of issuing the application.

Service is effected by fixing a copy of the documents to the main door or another conspicuous part of the premises and, if practicable, putting a copy in a transparent sealed envelope addressed to the occupier and posting it through the letterbox. In addition, copies can be fixed to stakes in the ground as for service of summary proceedings (see p. 116 above). However, this is not an alternative to fixing a copy to the main door.

The applicant must file an affidavit or witness statement of service in the prescribed form (N132) at or before the time fixed for the hearing of the application.

The hearing

This is conducted entirely on affidavit and can take place in either or both parties' absence. The respondent can only attend if he or she has filed an affidavit or witness statement in the prescribed form. Oral evidence cannot be given except in answer to direct questions from the court. It is therefore very important to file a detailed affidavit (see Chap. 16). After the hearing, the applicant can obtain a copy of the respondent's affidavit or witness statement from the court.

The interim order for possession

In deciding whether to make an order, the court considers whether the applicant has given or is prepared to give the following undertakings:

- if the court later holds that the applicant was not entitled to such an order:
  —to reinstate the respondent in the premises; and
  —to pay damages to the respondent; and
- pending final determination of the possession proceedings:
  —not to damage the premises;
  —not to grant a right of occupation to any other person; and

—not to damage or dispose of any of the respondent's possessions.

These undertakings are provided for in the prescribed form of the affidavit or witness statement.

The court must make an interim possession order if the applicant has filed an affidavit or witness statement of service, the court is satisfied that the conditions for the availability of an order are met (see above) and that any undertakings given by the applicant are adequate. The order must be in the prescribed form (N134).

An interim possession order provides that the respondent must vacate the premises within 24 hours of service. A return date is fixed by the court not less than seven days after the date of the order. The order expires on the return date.

The order must be served by the applicant in the same way as the notice of application (see above), together with the claim form and the applicant's affidavit (form N130), within 48 hours after the order has been approved by the judge. A further affidavit of service must be filed by the applicant before the return date (form N135). If this is not done, no further possession order can be made.

Effect of interim possession order

The effect of such an order is to create two offences (Criminal Justice and Public Order Act 1994, s. 76). The first is that it is an offence to trespass on the premises while the order is in force. An offence is not committed either by occupiers who leave within the 24-hour period or if a copy of the order was not fixed to the premises as set out above. Secondly, anyone who occupied the premises at the time of service of the order and then re-enters or attempts to re-enter the premises as a trespasser within a year of the date the order was served commits an offence.

The order cannot be enforced by a warrant of possession, so the applicant must ask the police to intervene by showing them a copy of the interim order and the affidavit of service to show that more than 24 hours have elapsed. A police officer in uniform may arrest anyone who is, or whom he or she reasonably suspects to be, guilty of either offence.

Where interim possession order is not granted

If the judge does not make an interim possession order, he or she gives directions for the matter to proceed, usually in accordance with the summary procedure under CPR Schedule 2, CCR Order 24 Part I. The court fixes a return date and serves the respondent with the claim form and affidavit in support.

The return date

The proceedings come back before the court on the return date for a final order to be made. The court may make a final order for possession, dismiss the claim for possession or give directions for the application to continue as summary proceedings under CPR Schedule 2, CCR Order 24 Part I as if no claim had been made for an interim possession order.

If the court dismisses the application and holds that the applicant was not entitled to an interim possession order, the respondent may apply to enforce any of the undertakings made by the applicant.

Timetable for interim possession order

This timetable assumes that the court lists any hearings as soon as it can and that the applicant takes as long as it can to fulfil its requirements.

Day 1: issue claim form with affidavit in support and notice of application.

Day 2: serve notice of application within 24 hours of issue; file affidavit of service before the hearing.

Day 5: hearing of application; order given.

Day 7: serve the interim possession order and claim form within 48 hours of the order being approved.

Day 8: occupiers must leave the property within 24 hours of the order being served to avoid committing an offence.

Day 13: return date for the claim form; final order.

Advantages and disadvantages

The advantages of interim possession proceedings are:

- Possession can be obtained within a few days.
- Possession can be obtained against unknown occupiers.
- The order can be enforced by the police.

The disadvantages are:

- There is no provision for a money claim.
- Possession can only be obtained against an outright trespasser or squatter.
- The landlord must act very quickly—within 28 days.
- The applicant must give undertakings which may be enforced if the interim possession order was wrongly obtained.
- The person swearing the affidavit or witness statement in support of the application is criminally liable for any false or misleading statement in the application.
- Many courts are very reluctant to make interim possession orders because of their Draconian nature.

12.
Injunctive Proceedings

Availability of injunctive proceedings / Commencing proceedings / The hearing / The order / Advantages and disadvantages

An injunction is a court order which directs someone to do or refrain from doing a particular act. An interlocutory injunction is one ordered before the final trial or judgment in proceedings. Injunctions are usually obtained after the court hears argument from both sides. However, in cases of real urgency a landlord may apply for an injunction without notifying the occupiers. An injunction can only be granted against known individuals as it is enforced by committal (i.e. sending to prison).

Injunctive proceedings in possession actions are most commonly used in cases of unlawful eviction to force a landlord to allow an occupier to reoccupy property. Before the introduction of interim possession orders, obtaining an injunction was the only way to remove trespassers from land before obtaining a final order for possession. Now its usefulness for landlords is confined to the following cases:

- where the landlord is not totally dispossessed (e.g. where known individuals make use of part of the property, perhaps by parking on it);
- cases of real urgency where there are identifiable trespassers.

Availability of injunctive proceedings

Proceedings can only be brought where the occupiers' identity is known. However, most unauthorised occupiers are unwilling to give their names. Yet where the occupiers appear to the court to form a sufficiently cohesive group, it is possible to bring representative proceedings if any of the occupiers' names are known, so that the known occupiers are appointed to represent the others. In those circumstances, the injunction cannot be enforced against the remaining unknown occupiers without the court's permission, but, on any application for permission, the court does not take account of any arguments by an unknown occupier that could have been raised by the representative party.

It is probably the case that injunctive proceedings cannot be brought against those who have the protection of section 3 of PEA 1977 (see Chap. 6).

An injunction will not be granted if it can be shown that the landlord has behaved oppressively in any way, or in such a way so as to mislead the occupiers into thinking they had permission to be on the premises.

Commencing proceedings

A landlord may seek an injunction as a final remedy. This is usual where it seeks to prevent further trespass to premises from which it has not been entirely dispossessed (e.g. to prevent unauthorised parking on its premises). Proceedings are issued and heard in the normal way. Where a landlord seeks an injunction as an interim measure, pending the hearing of proceedings for possession, it is necessary to apply for an interlocutory injunction.

An interlocutory injunction is a remedy obtained in the course of proceedings. It is not a final remedy. Therefore, unless sufficient urgency is shown, the main proceedings need to be issued before any application is made for an interim injunction. These proceedings usually include a claim for possession or an injunction or both. Therefore, the parties are known as claimant and defendant. In very urgent cases, usually on an application for an injunction without notice being given to the other side, it is possible to undertake to the court to issue proceedings as soon as practicable.

Ordinarily, applications for injunctions require at least two days' notice to the other side. Applications without notice can be heard very quickly. If the court office is told of the urgency, it is often possible to be listed that day.

The hearing

The hearing is usually before the judge rather than the district judge. The application must be supported by evidence, which can be set out in a witness statement, the statement of case or the application notice, provided that they are verified by a statement of truth. It is necessary to show the following:

- there is a serious issue to be tried; and
- the 'balance of convenience' is in the landlord's favour.

With regard to the latter, if it is clear that the occupiers have no right to be on the property, this is likely to be conclusive. However, if it appears that the occupier may have a defence, the court looks at whether damages would compensate the landlord or occupier adequately for refusing or granting the injunction. The court also tends to preserve the status quo. If the landlord can show a pressing need, such as one of health or safety, this weighs heavily in favour of granting an injunction.

If all the necessary evidence has not been filed by the hearing date, the court may grant an adjournment or dismiss the application. It is therefore important that the witness statement is as complete as possible to avoid unnecessary delay and expense.

Before an injunction is granted, the landlord is normally required to give an 'undertaking in damages'. This is a promise to the court to pay damages to the occupiers for any loss they suffer as a result of the injunction should it later appear that the landlord was not entitled to the injunction.

The order

An injunction is in the form that 'the defendant is forbidden from entering onto or remaining on the land owned by the claimant at [*address*] until [*date/further order*]'. If the injunction is made without notice being given to the occupiers, the occupiers can return to the court before the date specified to ask for the injunction to be discharged.

For the order to be enforceable, it must be served on the occupiers unless they are all present at the hearing and the court specifically orders that service is not required.

Although third parties cannot be bound by the injunction itself, it is a contempt of court either to aid or to abet any person named in the injunction to breach its terms or, knowing of the terms, to enter onto the land in question. Therefore, where an injunction is obtained, landlords should give the terms of the injunction wide publicity.

Advantages and disadvantages

The advantage is that an injunction can be obtained very quickly if it is sufficiently urgent. The disadvantages are:

- An interlocutory injunction is only an interim remedy. It is still necessary to proceed to trial of the issues.
- An injunction can only be obtained against known individuals. If further trespassers enter after proceedings are commenced, they must also be sued and made parties to the proceedings.
- Enforcement is by committal, which is a complex procedure.
- An injunction is probably not available against an occupier protected by section 3 of PEA 1977.

13. Ordinary Possession Proceedings

When ordinary proceedings are appropriate / Notices / Procedure / The order / Advantages and disadvantages

Where summary proceedings for possession are not appropriate, ordinary possession proceedings must be brought. Where interim injunctive relief is sought, the main action usually includes a claim for possession. Ordinary possession proceedings are available against all categories of occupier, providing the appropriate notices have been served.

When ordinary proceedings are appropriate

Ordinary possession proceedings are necessary if there is a complex issue of fact or law involved in establishing the landlord's claim to possession. If it appears in summary proceedings that a complex issue is raised as a defence, the judge will order that proceedings be continued as an ordinary possession action.

Ordinary proceedings are also necessary if the landlord wishes to include a money claim. This is usually damages for trespass or for use and occupation.

Notices

Before commencing ordinary possession proceedings, it is usually necessary to serve notice on the defendant (see Chap. 7). Where the defendant was a secure tenant or licensee, a notice under section 83 of HA 1985 is necessary; where the defendant was an assured tenant, a notice under section 8 of HA 1988 must be served; where the defendant was an assured shorthold tenant, notice in writing is required under section 21 of HA 1988. Where the defendant was a tenant with no security of tenure, a notice to quit is required to bring the tenancy to an end; a non-secure licence must be revoked by reasonable notice. In the usual case the landlord must give at least four-weeks' notice and the notice must be in the prescribed form. Where the occupier is a trespasser no notice is required, although any existing tenancy must have been brought to an end.

Service of notices

For any notice to be operative, it must be properly served. If an occupier can show that a notice addressed to him or her or to a tenant through whom he or she claims the right to be in the property was not properly served, this is a defence to possession proceedings (see Chap. 14).

Procedure

Proceedings are commenced by issuing a claim form under CPR Part 8, together with a particulars of claim. This is a formal document setting out the claimant's case and what the court is being asked to do. The particulars of claim must be verified by a statement of truth. The court will fix a hearing date and serve the proceedings on the occupiers. The occupiers may then file a defence, although they do not have to before the hearing.

Statement of truth

In the case of a corporate landlord, the statement of truth must be made by a director, treasurer, secretary, chief executive, manager or other officer of the company or corporation. Where the landlord is a local authority, the statement of truth may also be made by the mayor or other similar officer. In either case, the statement of truth can be made by the lawyer advising the landlord.

The statement of truth states: '[I believe] [The claimant believes] that the facts stated in this [particulars of claim] are true.'

If a person verifies a document containing a false statement without an honest belief in its truth, he or she can be found liable for contempt of court.

Hearing

The case comes before the court on the hearing date fixed by the court. If matters are relatively simple or the case is undefended, it may be decided then. If the case is more complex, the court gives directions for the management of the case. These may include directing the occupiers to file a defence, allocating the case to a track (depending on its complexity), ordering the parties to disclose documents and exchange of witness statements. If the occupiers have filed a defence already, the court will proceed to allocate the case to a track (see below).

Each party is under a duty to assist the court in allocation, and any other aspects of case management, and must be prepared to deal with any relevant matters any time the case comes before the court. It is important, therefore, that the parties are aware of all the issues, and the likely evidence, before the first hearing. Housing managers must ensure that their legal advisers are in possession of all relevant evidence as early as possible.

Allocation and case management

Possession actions can be allocated to the 'fast track' or the 'multi-track'. The main difference is that cases on the fast track are supposed to be capable of being dealt with in one day and the costs of the trial are fixed. In deciding which track to allocate the case to, the court has regard to the value of the claim, the complexity of the issues, the amount of oral evidence which may be required, the value and complexity of any Part 20 claim (i.e. any claim by the defendant against the claimant, e.g. for adverse possession) and the parties' wishes and circumstances. The court has extensive powers to restrict the amount of evidence that it will hear.

If the case is allocated to the fast track, a trial date is set at the outset, which the parties are required to work to. The trial date is normally within 30 weeks of directions being given. It will not be moved unless completely unavoidable. It is therefore important to comply with the intervening deadlines set by the court for various procedural stages and the court has powers to penalise any party who fails to do so (e.g. by ordering that they pay the costs of that stage or even by striking out their claim). It is essential therefore that housing managers respond as quickly as possible to requests from their legal advisers for information. This emphasises the importance of keeping good and well organised records so that all the relevant documents can be located within the relatively short time period which will be allowed for the preparation for trial.

Preparation for the trial

There are two main steps which will affect housing officers before trial. The first is disclosure of documents, and the second is preparing witness statements.

Disclosure of documents

Where the court orders the parties to disclose documents to each other, they must prepare lists of all the documents relevant to the case which they have or have had in their control. These include:

- the documents on which they rely, and
- any documents which:
  —adversely affect their case,
  —adversely affect another party's case, or
  —support another party's case.

Each party is under a duty to make a reasonable search for such documents. This is usually the task of the housing manager. If in any doubt whether a document should be disclosed, he or she should take legal advice.

Witness statements

A witness statement contains the evidence that the witness will give at trial. It must be verified by a statement of truth (see above). The witness statement must be as full as possible. At trial, the witness may only expand on the evidence in the statement with the court's permission, which will not be given unless there is a good reason to do so.

Housing officers need to ensure that their witness statements contain every relevant issue, but also that they are completely accurate. If the statement contains a false statement, the housing officer will be in contempt of court unless he or she honestly believed it to be true.

The order

If the court, having heard the case, decides to grant possession, the order is usually in the form that the defendants should give up possession to the claimant. Where the defendants were secure or assured tenants, the court has power to suspend the order as it thinks fit. Where the defendants entered the property as trespassers, the court has no power to suspend the order without the claimant's consent. In any other case, the county court only has power to suspend the date for possession for 14 days or, if to enforce the order sooner would cause exceptional hardship, for up to six weeks (HA 1980, s. 89). Exceptional hardship does not include the fact that the occupiers will be made homeless, although if they do not qualify for rehousing under Part VII of HA 1996, that could be a relevant consideration. In the High Court, this limitation does not apply, although possession should not normally be suspended for more than six weeks.

The order should also include any money claim by the claimant for arrears of rent, damages for trespass, use and occupation or mesne profits (see below).

The order for possession must be enforced by a warrant for possession in the county court or by a writ of possession in the High Court. This instructs the bailiffs to give possession of the property to the claimant and the bailiff can remove anybody who is present on the premises, whether or not they were parties to the proceedings (*R v Wandsworth County Court, ex p Wandsworth LBC* (1975)).

Money judgment

Where the defendant has been a tenant or licensee of the claimant, the claimant can ask for arrears of rent up to the date when the tenancy or licence ended. From that date until the date when possession is given up, the claimant is entitled to mesne profits (which are damages, usually at the rate at which rent or licence fees were charged on the property, for the defendant's use and occupation of the property).

Where the defendant is a trespasser, the claimant can claim damages for trespass which are normally assessed as the amount for which the premises could have been let during the period of trespass. These are often referred to as damages for use and occupation, although strictly speaking they are not. This amount can take into account any increases in rent which there would have been during the period of the defendant's occupation. Where an occupier was allowed into the property by a former tenant, he or she is liable for damages from the termination of the former tenancy, which is usually the date of expiry of a notice to quit. To recover arrears of rent on the former tenancy, the claimant must join the former tenant as a party to the proceedings.

Advantages and disadvantages

The advantages of ordinary possession proceedings are:

- It is possible to bring a money claim.
- It is more appropriate for assessing complex issues of fact and law.

The disadvantages are:

- The proceedings take longer and are more expensive.
- They must be brought against known defendants.

14.
Criminal Procedures

Offences committed by landlords / Offences committed by trespassers

Landlords must be aware of (and avoid committing) offences in trying to regain possession, and of the potential criminal remedies against unauthorised occupiers enforceable by arrest.

Offences committed by landlords

Section 1 of PEA 1977

Under section 1 it is an offence unlawfully to deprive or attempt to deprive a residential occupier of his or her occupation of any premises. A 'residential occupier' includes a tenant, licensee or any occupier protected by section 3 of PEA 1977 (see Chap. 6) which includes a former service occupier and former non-secure tenant. It does not include an excluded tenant or licensee whose tenancy or licence has expired.

The offence can be committed by a landlord in two main ways. The first is by actually depriving the occupier of the property (e.g. by changing the locks). The second is by:

1. doing anything which is likely to interfere with the peace and comfort of the occupier or his or her household, or

2. persistently withdrawing or withholding services reasonably required for occupyng the premises as a residence if the landlord knows or has reasonable cause to believe that the conduct is likely to cause the occupier to leave the premises.

The offence is usually prosecuted by the local authority; the maximum penalty is a fine and two years' imprisonment. Where the offence is committed by the local authority or a housing association, any officer whose position can be equated with that of a company director, manager or secretary can also be prosecuted personally if the offence was committed with his or her consent or because of his or her negligence.

Defences

It is a defence to show that the landlord had reasonable cause to believe and did actually believe that the residential occupier no longer lived at the premises. Where the complaint regards withdrawing or withholding services, it is a defence to show that the landlord had reasonable grounds for doing so. Such grounds might include non-payment of charges which specifically relate to provision of the services in question or the necessity to withhold services to carry out essential repair to plant or installations.

Section 6 of the Criminal Law Act (CLA) 1977

It is an offence under this section for any person knowingly to use or threaten violence to secure entry to premises if there is someone present on the premises who is opposed to the entry. 'Someone present' includes an outright trespasser being evicted by the person entitled to possession. Violence includes violence to property (e.g. smashing a window or forcing the lock). 'Premises' is widely defined to include immovable structures, moveable structures adapted for residential purposes and ancillary land.

Defence

There is a statutory defence which provides that no offence is committed by 'displaced residential occupiers', 'protected intending occupiers' or their agents.

A 'displaced residential occupier' (DRO) is a person who lawfully occupied premises as his or her residence immediately before he or she was excluded from the premises by a person who entered the premises as a trespasser. A person remains a DRO for as long as he or she is excluded from the property by the original or any subsequent trespassers.

'Protected intending occupiers' (PIOs) include tenants or licensees of a local authority or a registered housing association who require the premises for their own occupation as a residence and are excluded from the premises by a person who entered the premises as a trespasser. A PIO must have a certificate stating his or her right to occupy the premises and that the tenancy or licence was granted by the authority or association. It is an offence for anyone to make a false statement in the certificate which he or she knows to be false or without giving due thought about whether it is true or false.

This defence is available to housing officers only if they are acting as agents of DROs or PIOs. Given the potential physical dangers of direct physical repossession, it is advisable to use the procedures against trespassers under section 7 of CLA 1977 (see pp. 141–143 below).

Dangers of direct physical repossession

The above offences demonstrate the dangers to social landlords of attempting direct physical repossession, apart from the danger of physical violence to their employees. First, the landlord must be certain of the occupier's status. If the landlord takes direct physical action to evict an occupier who later turns out to have statutory protection, not only the landlord but any officers involved in the eviction will be criminally liable. Secondly, even if the occupiers are known to be trespassers, there are stringent limitations on the use of force to regain possession. Such action can only be taken when the property is empty. Many squatters are aware of this limitation and ensure that there is always someone on the premises. In these circumstances, it is always advisable to take court proceedings against the occupiers so as to safeguard the landlord's interests.

Offences committed by trespassers

Section 7 of CLA 1977

Anyone who enters and remains on premises as a trespasser commits an offence if he or she fails to leave on being required to do so by or on behalf of a DRO or a PIO. An offence is committed by any person allowed onto the premises by a trespasser. The police can arrest without a warrant anyone who is guilty or whom they reasonably suspect to be guilty of the offence.

Defences

There are three defences to the offence under section 7:

- if the trespasser can show he or she believed the person requiring him or her to leave was not, nor was acting on behalf of, a DRO or a PIO;
- where the person requiring the trespasser to leave claimed to be, or to be acting on behalf of, a PIO and failed to produce a certificate (see p. 140 above) on request;
- if the premises are mainly non-residential and the trespasser was not in any part used for residential purposes.

To avoid direct confrontation between a DRO or PIO and trespassers, it is usual for housing officers to undertake the responsibility of requiring the trespassers to leave on the DRO or PIO's behalf. It is important for officers to have the necessary authorisation from the DRO or PIO and, in the case of a PIO, to be able to produce on demand the certificate that the occupier is a PIO.

Once the trespassers are required to leave the premises, the police can be called to remove them. This is clearly preferable to any direct action under section 6 of CLA 1977 (see p. 140 above) as it avoids confrontation. In most cases it is unnecessary for the police to arrest the trespassers and they will leave peaceably.

Protected intending occupiers

Enforcing the criminal remedies under section 7 of CLA 1977 can be a very quick way of repossessing a PIO's premises occupied by trespassers. The procedure is principally designed for the situation where a tenant has accepted a tenancy of a property which is then occupied by a trespasser before the tenant has moved in.

Some local authorities have used this procedure to offer property already squatted to homeless families who are then issued with PIO certificates; possession is regained by the local authority on their behalf and the family is allowed into occupation once the property is repaired. However, note that the tenancy must not be granted solely as a means of regaining possession of the premises: the normal allocation procedures must be followed. There must actually be a PIO who has given the landlord authority to act on his or her behalf. Therefore, the occupier must have a tenancy before action can be taken against the trespassers. Difficulties can arise, particularly with homelessness. If the property is squatted, it is usually impossible to ascertain its suitability, as is necessary under the homelessness legislation. If the PIOs are allowed to reject the premises once they can gain access to it, there may be no tenancy until the premises' suitability is confirmed. In that case, the prospective tenants would not have been PIOs at the time of repossession, which would be an abuse of section 7 and thus provide the trespassers with a defence. The landlord further runs risks of committing an offence by completing a certificate that the tenants are PIOs when in fact they are not, and having a finding of maladministration against it.

Given these risks and the swiftness of the interim possession order procedure (see Chap. 11), it is preferable to pursue the civil remedies rather than use section 7 in these circumstances.

Case report

A and B, who were squatting a council property, brought a complaint against Tower Hamlets LBC. The tenant, Mrs F, informed the council that the property was squatted, that she wanted to terminate her tenancy and hand over the keys. The estate officer asked Mrs F to sign an authorisation requesting the council to act on her behalf to regain possession. He also issued her with a certificate that she was a PIO. A and B were required to leave and the police were called.

The Local Government Ombudsman found that there had been maladministration. Mrs F was not a PIO. If anything, she was a DRO. Therefore there was no legal basis for A and B's eviction. He concluded that the failure to comply with section 7 of CLA 1977 arose because the officers had not been properly trained how to use the legislation. *Investigation into Complaint 88/A/858 against Tower Hamlets LBC*

Key points

- It is an offence unlawfully to deprive or attempt to deprive a residential occupier of his or her occupation of any premises (PEA 1977, s. 1).
- It is an offence knowingly to use or threaten violence to gain entry to premises if there is someone present who opposes the entry. No offence is committed by a DRO or a PIO (CLA 1977, s. 6).
- Anyone who enters and remains on premises as a trespasser commits an offence if he or she fails to leave after a DRO or a PIO has required him or her to do so (CLA 1977, s. 7).

15.
Private and Public Law Defences

Private law defences / Public law defences / Other defences

This chapter looks at the defences to proceedings commonly raised by unauthorised occupiers. It also deals with what housing managers can do both as matters of general housing management and in preparing proceedings to counter these defences.

Defences raised by unauthorised occupiers fall into two main categories: private law and public law. There are also defences specific to the type of proceedings being brought.

Private law defences

There are three main types. The first is where the housing association or local authority has no entitlement (or *standing*) to sue (i.e. the landlord is not the appropriate person to bring possession proceedings).The second is where the unauthorised occupiers were granted a tenancy or licence either directly by the housing association or local authority, or because the previous tenant granted the occupiers a subtenancy (whether legal or illegal) and has since surrendered his or her own tenancy. The third is where the unauthorised occupiers become the owners of the property by means of *adverse possession* (see pp. 150–153 below).

No standing to sue

Failure to terminate previous tenancy

Possession proceedings can only be brought by someone who is immediately entitled to possession. Where premises are let to a tenant and later occupied by unauthorised occupiers, only the tenant is immediately entitled to possession. The landlord cannot bring possession proceedings until it has terminated the tenancy and has itself acquired an immediate right to possession. It is therefore a defence for an unauthorised occupier to show that there is a tenancy which has not been determined.

There are three main situations which commonly confront housing managers:

- the tenant has left the property;
- the tenant has attempted to determine the tenancy;
- the tenant has died.

(See further Chap. 8.) Care must be taken in all these situations and the correct procedure followed before the landlord can demonstrate conclusively that the tenancy has in fact ended.

Applicants are merely licensees

A licensee, unlike a tenant, does not have an interest in the land. A licence simply gives permission for the licensee to use the land. Traditionally, this has meant that licensees could not bring proceedings for possession against trespassers unless the trespassers had actually dispossessed them. Unlawful occupiers have successfully resisted proceedings brought in the name of the licensee, arguing that they should have been brought in the name of the person granting the licence.

This position has been altered by *Manchester Airport plc v Dutton* (see 'Case report' below). The position now is that, if the trespasser's occupation interferes with the terms of the applicant's licence, the applicant may apply to the court for a summary possession order.

This is particularly relevant in the case of short-life housing agreements whereby the local authority grants a licence of property earmarked for development to a housing association to let on short-term licences until the development actually takes place. It is usually the case that any trespass on the property interferes substantially with the housing association's rights under the licence and the association can therefore bring possession proceedings in its own name.

Case report

A wood owned by the National Trust was close to the proposed second runway for Manchester Airport. To comply with the conditions of operation of the runway, the airport company had to reduce the height of any obstacles in the flight path, which included felling or lopping trees in the wood. The National Trust gave the company a licence to carry out the works, but the wood was occupied by trespassers opposed to the works on ecological grounds. Although the trespassers were occupying National Trust land, the Trust did not wish to be involved in any action against them. The airport company therefore sought an order for possession of the wood.

The Court of Appeal, by a majority, held that the court had power to grant a remedy to a licensee which would protect, but not exceed, the rights granted by the licence. Thus, a licensee not in possession of land could claim possession against a trespasser if that was a necessary remedy to give effect to the rights of occupation he or she enjoyed under the licence. It would be a question of fact in every case whether the trespass interfered with those rights. If an order for possession was the only practical remedy, as in this case, that remedy should be granted. *Manchester Airport plc v Dutton* (1999)

Creation of tenancy or licence

Occupiers commonly assert that they were granted a tenancy or licence by the landlord and that this has not been properly determined. Usually they claim that they have gained security of tenure as a result, which makes it much more difficult to repossess the premises. Occupiers may claim that the previous tenant assigned his or her tenancy to them before leaving.

Tenancy created by landlord

It is for the occupier to show that he or she was given a tenancy. To do this he or she must show that
- the previous tenancy has been determined;
- to the landlord's knowledge, he or she has been paying rent on his or her own behalf and not as the previous tenant's agent.

The occupier's ability to show that the previous tenancy has been determined depends on the circumstances. If the occupier can show that the previous tenant has abandoned the property and the landlord was aware of this, he or she will argue that by granting him or her a new tenancy, the landlord has accepted that the previous tenancy has ended by surrender by operation of law. If there has been a possession order in relation to the previous tenancy, the occupier will argue that the previous tenancy came to an end either because the order was an outright order, in which case the tenancy will have ended on the date specified in the order for possession to be given up, or because the previous tenant breached the terms of a suspended order, in which case the tenancy will have ended immediately the order was breached.

To show that the landlord has granted him or her a new tenancy, the occupier first needs to show that the landlord was aware of his or her occupation, and secondly that it has acted so as to accept him or her as tenant. He or she commonly points to the acceptance of rent or the landlord's carrying out of repairs at the occupier's request as evidence that the landlord has accepted him or her as a tenant. In itself, however, this is not sufficient to show that a tenancy has been granted: the occupiers could, quite simply, be acting on the tenant's behalf. There is no obligation on a tenant to pay his or her rent or report repairs personally. Especially where the tenant is temporarily absent from the property, it is not uncommon for those who occupy the premises on his or her behalf to pay the rent for him or her. The occupier has to show, therefore, that he or she was paying rent on his or her own behalf and that the landlord was aware of this (*Tower Hamlets LBC v Ayinde* (1994)).

In order to show this, an occupier may rely on conversations he or she claims were held with a housing officer in which he or she made it clear that he or she wanted the tenancy. The occupier should be asked to identify the housing officer in question, whether by name or description. To establish the truth of such claims, it may be possible to show that no-one fitting the occupier's description was employed by the relevant housing office at the time. However, it may be that the housing officer has left the landlord's employment or does not remember the alleged conversation. It is therefore very important that officers keep good notes of any interviews with unauthorised occupiers of property and that they are kept in such a way that they are not lost.

If such a conversation does occur, it is very important that action is taken. It should immediately be made clear to the occupier, in writing, that the landlord does not accept him or her as a tenant and that any payments made by him or her will be accepted for use and occupation only. If possession proceedings are not commenced immediately, the officer must ensure that no subsequent dealings between the occupier and the housing office could give rise to allegations that the landlord has given the occupier a tenancy. If the situation is allowed to drag on, it may be argued by the occupier that, despite initially saying that the landlord does not accept him or her as a tenant, by accepting payments and failing to take any proceedings, the landlord has accepted him or her as a tenant.

Local authorities should also beware as, if a licence or permission is given to an occupier allowing him or her to remain in exclusive occupation, that licence itself becomes secure and the authority can only take possession proceedings on the grounds set out in HA 1985 (see Chap. 7). The only exceptions to this are where the statutory exceptions to security apply (HA 1985, Sched. 1) or the licence is given as a temporary expedient to someone who entered the premises as a trespasser (HA 1985, s. 79(3)). Therefore, the longer the local authority accepts the occupier's presence, the easier it is for the occupier to show that he or she has at least been granted a licence.

An occupier may also argue that because he or she has received housing benefit for that property, the local authority has accepted him or her as a tenant. This argument does not necessarily stand up because it is not only tenants who are eligible for housing benefit. Some housing benefit departments state on their forms that granting housing benefit does not imply granting a tenancy. It all depends on the circumstances of the case. However, where it has been made clear to the occupier in writing that the local authority requires him or her to move out, merely granting a housing benefit application does not result in granting a tenancy (*Westminster City Council v Basson* (1990)).

Assignment by previous tenant

An occupier may assert that the previous tenant assigned the tenancy to him or her (see Chap. 8). A housing manager needs to ask two questions:

- Is this a situation where an assignment is possible?
- Is the assignment in writing?

If the answer to either of these questions is 'No', the occupier usually has no defence. If it is a situation where an assignment is possible and the assignment was in writing, the assignment may still have required the landlord's consent. If this has not been obtained, the assignment is valid, but it may be possible to bring possession proceedings on the ground that there has been a breach of the tenancy conditions.

Creation of a licence

Occupiers often claim to have been granted a licence using some or all of the following arguments:

- the landlord is aware of their presence in the property, whether directly or as, for example, a result of the occupiers paying council tax for that property, but has not previously required them to leave;
- the landlord has done repairs to the property, knowing that they were in occupation;
- they have applied to the local authority landlord for housing but their application has not been processed. In the circumstances, the local authority must be taken to have granted them a licence to continue occupying the property.

Even if an occupier can establish the facts to support one of these arguments, it is not conclusive. Just because a landlord does not immediately require a trespasser to leave on discovering his or her presence, there is no necessary implication that he or she has permission to remain there. If a landlord does not wish to take possession proceedings immediately, it is advisable to write to the occupier making it clear that he or she is in occupation without the landlord's permission. As for repairs, if the landlord carries out specific repairs at the occupier's request, this may indicate its willingness for him or her to remain. Yet it may equally be attributable to the landlord's own wish to maintain the property or to prevent the property from becoming dangerous and giving rise to a potential liability under the Occupier's Liability Acts (see Chap. 4). As to the local authority's duties to process homelessness applications, these are completely unconnected to its function as a landlord. Thus there is no basis for implying any licence.

Adverse possession

What is adverse possession

A very important defence which may be raised by unauthorised occupiers is that of adverse possession. This can happen where a property has been occupied for a period of 12 years or more by individuals who can show that they never had permission to be there and who intended to take possession of the property. The previous owner's title to the property is then extinguished and the occupiers become the lawful owners of the property.

This happens most commonly where a landlord (often a local authority) has acquired land or premises in order to carry out a major development programme which may have to wait for funding or planning permission. In the meantime, the land usually lies empty, giving an opportunity for others to take it over and use it themselves.

To establish adverse possession, the occupiers have to show that:

- the true owner has either given up possession of the land or been dispossessed; and
- they had been in adverse possession of the land for more than 12 years before the action was brought.

The occupiers must show that they were openly occupying the land and that they did not have the landlord's permission to enter or remain on the premises. The occupation must also have been 'adverse' to the landowner. This means that the occupiers must have had the intention to possess the property for themselves. They must have dealt with the property as an occupying owner would have done and they must be able to show that no-one else has done so, for example by fencing the land or changing the locks. If, however, the true owner was prevented by law from seeking possession, the defence does not apply (*Smith v Lawson* (1997)).

The period of continuous adverse possession must be 12 years or more. It is not necessary, however, that the possession is by the same people for all that time as long as a continuous period of adverse possession can be established over 12 years.

Steps to be taken

When a landlord discovers that his property is subject to adverse possession, it is very important that steps are taken immediately to terminate it. Otherwise the landlord risks what is essentially giving away valuable property to the occupiers.

Once adverse possession has been established, it can be terminated either by the landlord granting permission for the possession, in which case it is no longer 'adverse', or by the landlord actually recovering possession himself. It is important to note, however, that merely writing a letter to the occupiers informing them that the landlord objects to their occupation is *not* sufficient to stop the possession being adverse. Some positive action must be taken.

One option open to the landlord is to grant the occupiers a licence. Where a licence is granted as a temporary expedient to persons who entered the premises as trespassers, it is neither secure (HA 1985, s. 79(4)) nor protected by PEA 1977 (s. 3A(6)). For these purposes, it is probably sufficient if the landlord writes to the occupants granting them a licence to occupy the premises and they do not reply refusing to accept such a licence (*BP Properties Ltd v Buckler* (1987)).

Adverse possession is interrupted if any person in possession acknowledges the landowner's title. An acknowledgement must be in writing and signed by the person making it. The 12 years in which the landlord must bring possession proceedings starts again from the date of the acknowledgement. The landlord could require the signing of an acknowledgement as a condition for not commencing immediate possession proceedings.

Alternatively, the landlord must bring possession proceedings. The quickest way is usually to take summary proceedings (see Chap. 10). It is open to the landlord to bring proceedings for an interim possession order in the county court as long as it could not reasonably have known about the occupation more than 28 days before the application is made (see Chap. 11).

Example

Aberham BC owns Primrose Cottage. In 1973 it was empty. Mary broke in and started to live there. She changed the locks and treated the property as her home. In 1979, however, the council realised that she was occupying the property. Threatening her with eviction, it persuaded her to sign an acknowledgement that it was the true owner of the property. The council did not, however, take any further action, nor did it give her any permission to stay there. In 1983, she decided to move away and let her friend Silas live in the property. In 1988, the council again realised that the property was being occupied without its consent. It therefore sent a letter to Silas requiring him to leave the premises within 14 days. In 1989, the council started legal proceedings but had to withdraw them because they were defective. Finally, in 1993, the council brought possession proceedings. Silas successfully defended the proceedings on the basis that the council's title had been extinguished and that he was now the freehold owner of Primrose Cottage. The limitation period ran from the date when Mary signed the acknowledgement. Since then, there had been 14 years of adverse possession which was not broken by the council sending a letter demanding possession, nor by the unsuccessful issuing of proceedings in 1989.

Public law defences

A public law defence is only usually available against local authority landlords and even then is quite limited in its operation. It can be a defence that the decision by the local authority to institute proceedings was unreasonable. This can arise when an occupier alleges that the local authority owes him or her a duty, that the local authority has failed to fulfil its duty, that the breach of duty has led to the occupier being a trespasser and that therefore the decision to evict is unreasonable while the authority remains in breach. The county court does not have power to decide whether the authority has acted reasonably. The occupier should ask for an adjournment so that he or she can seek judicial review of the decision to bring proceedings in the first place. Permission must obtained be from the High Court before the occupier can bring judicial review proceedings. The county court judge, in making the decision whether to adjourn, must consider the likelihood of success in the application for leave for judicial review (*Avon CC v Buscott* (1988)).

Provided that an unauthorised occupier has nowhere else to live, he or she will almost certainly be considered homeless. Occupiers often allege that they have applied to the local authority as homeless and that the authority has failed to process the application. They therefore seek to adjourn proceedings to apply for judicial review. More often than not this is a delaying tactic. It has been decided, however, that there is no duty on a local authority to determine whether a person is homeless before deciding whether to take possession proceedings (*R v Barnet LBC, ex p Grumbridge* (1992)). Therefore the application for judicial review is bound to fail and an adjournment should not be granted.

Other defences

Summary possession proceedings

It is a defence to proceedings under CPR Schedule 2, CCR Order 24 Part I for the occupier to show that he is a tenant holding over after the end of his tenancy. Proceedings then have to be recommenced using the normal possession procedure.

Interim possession procedures

It is a defence to an application for an interim possession order for the occupiers to show that:

1. the landlord could reasonably have known about their occupation more than 28 days before proceedings were issued, either by virtue of direct observation or by records (e.g. held by the homeless persons unit) showing the premises as their address;

2. they did not enter the land as trespassers but were let in by the previous tenant, licensee or owner.

Any occupier wishing to raise these matters in his or her defence must file an affidavit before the hearing.

16.
Preparing Possession Proceedings

The housing officer's role / Affidavits and witness statements

Housing managers have several, crucial roles in possession proceedings. This chapter looks at what they are and how housing officers can carry them out effectively. Further guidance on preparing possession proceedings can be found in A. Dymond, *Presenting Possession Proceedings* (Arden's Housing Library, 1996).

The housing officer's role

It is usually housing officers who, on behalf of the landlord, take action to terminate any tenancy of the property and who have direct dealings with the unauthorised occupiers. It is on these dealings that occupiers rely to support allegations that they have been granted a tenancy or licence.

The housing officer is also the person responsible for gathering evidence. It is therefore very important that good and complete records are kept of all transactions with the property; reference to old records can stretch back 20 years or more. There should be a filing system where old records cannot be lost or damaged.

When proceedings are contemplated, it is essential that there is effective communication between the housing office and the legal advisers over what evidence is available and exactly what has taken place. This helps the advisers to know what type of proceedings are appropriate and what further evidence, if any, is required.

The housing officer is responsible for giving evidence in support of the possession proceedings, whether orally in court or in the form of an affidavit or witness statement. The form and contents of affidavits and witness statements is dealt with below.

Affidavits and witness statements

A witness statement contains the evidence that a witness wishes to give. It is not made on oath, but must be verified by a statement of truth. It is a contempt of court to make a false statement in a witness statement without an honest belief in its truth. A witness statement should exhibit any documents relied on.

Witness statements are the primary method by which the court receives evidence in writing. They may be used in summary and interim possession proceedings and other interim applications. If a claim for possession is contested and goes to trial, witness statements must be exchanged in advance. While the witnesses must give oral evidence at the trial unless the court orders otherwise, so that they can be cross-examined, the witness statement usually stands as the whole of the evidence. The court only allows a witness to expand on the evidence in the statement if there is a good reason to do so. It is therefore very important for such statements to be as full as possible.

In contrast, an affidavit is a sworn statement containing a witness's evidence. Evidence must be on affidavit if required by the court, but, in practice, this is rarely necessary. A party may choose to put in affidavit evidence instead of witness statements, but cannot recover any extra costs of doing so. Affidavits are not usually used at trials, except to prove the service of documents such as notices to quit, although, if service is disputed, the relevant officer is usually required to attend court.

Evidence in summary and interim possession proceedings

In summary and interim proceedings, evidence is in writing. In interim possession proceedings, no evidence may be adduced that is not included in the affidavit or witness statement, which must be in the prescribed form (N130). Housing officers must ensure that their affidavit or statement contains all the information on which the landlord wishes to rely.

In summary proceedings, the landlord must show that it is entitled to possession of the premises by:

- showing that it has title to the property and that it is entitled to immediate possession;
- stating that there is no tenant or licensee who is entitled to possession;
- where relevant, giving details of how any previous tenancy came to an end;
- explaining the circumstances in which the premises came to be occupied by strangers without its consent; and
- stating that it does not know the name of any person occupying the land who is not named in the claim form.

Once the landlord has shown that it has title, it is for the unauthorised occupier to prove any right he or she has to remain in the property (*Portland Managements Ltd v Harte* (1977)).

The affidavit or statement should provide sufficient detail that the court is content to rely on it. Any documents referred to should be attached as exhibits.

To prove the landlord's title, copies of the Land Registry entries for the premises should be exhibited. The affidavit or statement should confirm that they are true copies. If the title is a complicated one where the attached plan uses different colours to mark out different areas, the colours must be marked on any copies so that the judge can identify which areas belong to the landlord. It is also possible to prove the landlord's title by exhibiting a copy of the conveyance by which it acquired its title (e.g. a copy of the lease). A local authority which acquired title to land after a reorganisation of local government may have to prove title by producing the statutory instrument under which title to the land passed.

The circumstances in which the property came to be occupied without the landlord's consent will vary from case to case. Where the occupiers were licensees, the statement or affidavit must show that the licence has been properly revoked, exhibiting any revocation of licence. Similarly, if the occupiers were allowed onto the premises by the former tenant, their right to remain ends when the tenancy ends. The landlord must show that this has happened, exhibiting any necessary documentation (e.g. a notice to quit).

The statement or affidavit should contain information about the housing officer's investigations which led to the discovery that the occupiers were on the land and the evidence he or she has collected to show that they have no right to be there.

A statement or affidavit can contain hearsay statements. These are written or verbal statements made outside court, the contents of which are relied on to prove the case (e.g. a neighbour's statement to the housing officer that the tenant has left the property). The source of any hearsay statement must be identified.

If evidence is given by affidavit, it must be sworn or affirmed. This involves the housing officer in whose name the affidavit is written taking it, and any exhibits, to a solicitor (not the landlord's solicitor) or commissioner for oaths or to an officer of the court and swearing or affirming that the contents of the affidavit are true.

Example form of witness statement

Applicant
Witness: S Officer
1st witness statement
Exhibits: SO1, SO2
Date: 6th May 1999

IN THE NORCHESTER COUNTY COURT Case No

BETWEEN

NORCHESTER DISTRICT COUNCIL Applicants

and

(1) MICHAEL JONES
(2) PERSONS UNKNOWN Respondents

STATEMENT OF SALLY OFFICER

1. My full name is Sally Ann Officer. I am a housing officer employed by the applicant at the Norchester District Housing Office, Riverside, Norchester, NO1 23P. I have responsibility for the management of premises at 14A Long Lane, Norchester NO7 89Q (the 'premises'). I am duly authorised by the applicant to make this statement in support of the applicant's claim for possession of the premises.

2. The applicant is the [freehold] [leasehold] owner of the premises. There is now produced and shown to me and exhibited herewith marked SO1 a true copy of the Land Registry entry in relation to title no. [*insert title no.*], showing the applicant's title to the premises.

3. There is no tenant or licensee of the applicant who is entitled to possession of the premises. [*Insert here, if necessary, details of the determination of the interest of any previous tenant/licensee, e.g.* The previous tenant, Mr Sam Brown, was transferred to another property owned by the applicant on 3rd June 1998. He moved out of the premises and returned the keys to the housing office on that date.]

4. [*Circumstances in which property came to be occupied without applicant's consent, e.g.*] On 12th March 1999, in the course of routine inspections of the applicant's properties, I noticed that there were persons in occupation of the premises. I knocked on the door and it was answered by a man who gave the name Michael Jones. I could see that there were other persons in occupation whose names are not known to me or to the applicant. I asked the occupants how they came to be in occupation of the premises but they refused to answer.

5. I then called on Mr Ron Smith, the tenant of 14B Long Lane, which is the flat directly above the premises. He informed me that he had noticed the occupiers of the premises moving in about three weeks earlier.

6. From the applicant's records, I believe that at no time has the applicant given permission for anyone to occupy the premises.

7. [*Revocation of consent*] On 13th March 1999, I delivered at the premises a notice informing the occupiers that they were occupying the premises without the applicant's consent, that any licence which they may have had was thereby revoked, that any payments made by them would be accepted as damages for trespass only and that they should vacate the premises by 1st April 1999. A true copy of the notice is now produced and shown to me and exhibited herewith marked SO2.

8. On 2nd April 1999, I visited the premises and rang the bell. No-one answered but I could see through the window signs that the premises were still being occupied.

9. The applicant does not know the name of any person in occupation of the premises who is not already named in the claim form.

10. [*Statement of truth*] I believe that the facts stated in this witness statement are true.

Signed ____________

Dated: 6th May 1999

Part V

Occupation of Open Land

17. Removal Directions and Orders

Removal direction / Removal orders

There has been a perception that trespass on or occupation of open land by gypsies, new-age travellers and protesters is on the increase. As a result, local authorities and the police were given wide-ranging powers to deal with it in the Criminal Justice and Public Order Act (CJPOA) 1994. Local authorities can issue removal directions, which are then enforced by magistrates making removal orders; the police can require the occupiers to leave open land where certain conditions are satisfied. These new remedies are mostly confined to dealing with trespass on open land. It is therefore not appropriate to use them where the occupation complained of is of buildings. They can be used where the trespassers' names are unknown and also operate to prevent re-entry onto the land.

The summary possession procedure under CPR Schedule 2, CCR Order 24 and Schedule 1, RSC Order 113 can be used where the premises are open land; however, the interim possession procedure is confined to buildings and so cannot be used (see further Chap. 11). Injunctive proceedings are available, but only if the trespassers' identities are known.

Whilst this Part may seem to be directed mostly at local authorities, it is important for the housing managers of other social landlords to be aware of these remedies. They will then be in a position either to call in the police or to request the assistance of the local authority when any open land in their ownership is occupied without their consent.

Removal direction

This is a direction given by the local authority under section 77 of CJPOA 1994 to persons residing in vehicles on certain types of land, and which requires those persons to leave. Once a direction is given, it is an offence for them to remain on the land or to re-enter within three months.

The power to make removal directions only applies to open land and not to buildings. It applies to

- land forming part of a highway;
- any other unoccupied land;
- any occupied land where the persons reside there without the occupier's consent.

Persons subject to the direction

A removal direction can be directed to any persons whom the local authority considers to be residing in a vehicle or vehicles for the time being within the local authority area on any of the types of land set out above. A 'vehicle' in this context includes:

- any vehicle, whether or not it is in a fit state for use on roads;
- any body, whether or not it has wheels, which appears to have formed part of such a vehicle;
- any load carried by, and anything attached to, such a vehicle; and
- a caravan, whether or not it is itself motorised or is towed by or carried on another vehicle.

Persons can be regarded as 'residing' on any land despite the fact that they may have a home elsewhere.

Considerations when making a removal direction

As with any local authority decision, the authority must take into account all the relevant circumstances when deciding whether to make a removal direction. There is specific guidance which was produced by the then DoE (now the DETR) in relation to gypsies which must be taken into consideration. There are parts of that guidance which have been termed 'considerations of common humanity' and therefore apply in all cases when a removal direction is being considered, whether or not gypsies are involved:

> 10. Social services departments and local housing authorities are reminded of their obligations under Part III of the Children Act 1989 (Local Authority Support for Children and Families); and Part III of the Housing Act 1985 (Housing the Homeless) [now HA 1996, Part VII]. The Secretaries of State expect authorities to take careful account of these obligations when taking decisions about the future maintenance of authorised gypsy caravan sites and the eviction of persons from unauthorised sites.
>
> 11. Local education authorities should bear in mind their statutory duty to make appropriate educational provision available for all school-age children in their area, whether resident temporarily or permanently. ... [T]his duty embraces traveller children. Local education authorities should take careful account of the effects of an eviction on the education of children already enrolled, or in the process of being enrolled, at a school. Where an authority decides to proceed with an eviction, and any families concerned move elsewhere in the same area, alternative educational arrangements must be made in accordance with the requirements of the law appropriate to the children's ages, abilities and aptitudes.
>
> 12. The Secretaries of State also expect local authorities who decide to proceed with evictions to liaise with other local authorities who may have statutory responsibilities to discharge in respect of those persons who are being evicted.

> 13. Local authorities should also bear in mind that families camped unlawfully on land may need or may be receiving assistance from local health or welfare services. When they have decided to proceed with an eviction, they should liaise with the relevant statutory agencies, particularly where pregnant women or newly-born children are involved, to ensure that those agencies are not prevented from fulfilling their obligations towards these persons.

(DoE Circular 18/94: *Gypsy Sites Policy and Unauthorised Camping*.)

The authority must therefore take into consideration the trespassers' needs and balance those against the needs of local residents (*R v Wealden DC, ex p Wales; R v Same, ex p Stratford; R v Lincolnshire CC, ex p Atkinson* (1995)).

Gypsies

Gypsies have a distinct cultural identity which tends to conflict with many of the values of modern life. Yet it is generally recognised that they must be allowed to continue what is a traditional way of life and that, where necessary, provision must be made for them. Gypsies, in law, are people who have a nomadic habit of life in making or seeking their livelihood (*R v South Hams DC, ex p Gibb* (1994)). Their race and origin do not matter. Members of an organised group of travelling showmen or people in travelling circuses are not classed as gypsies. New-age travellers or other groups of people who travel from area to area are not classed as gypsies unless they can show that they travel to find employment.

It has long been recognised that gypsies need somewhere to place their caravans and this resulted in legislation in the late 1960s requiring local authorities to provide sites for them to prevent them being continually moved on. This duty was, however, repealed by the CJPOA 1994 and local authorities now merely have the power to provide such sites together with areas where gypsies can carry out their work.

Considerations relating to gypsies
Despite the repeal of the duty to provide sites, the then DoE issued guidance on the ways in which authorities should exercise their powers to issue removal directions against gypsies (DoE Circular No 18/94—see pp. 167–168 above). It states that local authorities should not evict gypsies needlessly; the power to issue removal directions should be used in a humane and compassionate way, primarily to reduce nuisance. Where gypsies are encamped on local authority land and are not causing a nuisance, in general they should be allowed to remain there for a short period unless there is a nearby local authority site which they refuse to use. When authorities decide to allow gypsies to remain on such sites, they should consider providing basic facilities for sanitation, rubbish disposal and the provision of drinking water to minimise the level of nuisance that may be caused.

Service

Once the local authority has decided to make a removal direction, it must be served on the individuals concerned. It can merely specify the land concerned and be addressed to all occupants of the vehicles on the land. It need not name the individual occupiers.

A direction should be served personally on any named occupant. Where it is not practicable to serve him or her personally, it is sufficient to fix a copy of it in a prominent place on the vehicle concerned. Where the direction is addressed to unnamed occupants, it should be served by fixing a copy of it in a prominent place to every vehicle on the land at the time of service.

The local authority is under a duty to take such steps as may be reasonably practicable to ensure that a copy of the direction is displayed on the land (other than by being fixed to a vehicle) in such a way that it is likely to be seen by any person camping on the land.

The authority must also give notice of the direction to the landowner and any occupier unless, after reasonable inquiries, the authority cannot ascertain their name and address.

Effect of removal direction

A removal direction requires the persons to whom it is directed, and any others with them, to leave the land, and remove their vehicles and any other property they have with them on the land.

A person who knows that a removal direction has been given which applies to him or her commits an offence if he or she:

- fails, as soon as practicable, to leave the land or remove any vehicle or other property which is the subject of the direction; or
- having removed vehicles or property again enters the land with a vehicle within three months beginning with the day on which the direction was given.

This is a summary offence (which can only be tried in the magistrates' court). The maximum fine is currently £1,000.

To prosecute such an offence, the local authority must 'lay an information' at the court which then issues and serves a summons. An information is a statement by the person who wishes to bring a prosecution (in this case the officer of the local authority who has the authority to bring prosecutions in the authority's name) of the alleged offence with which the person accused is to be charged. An information must not allege more than one offence: a separate information must be used for each. An information must be laid within six months of the offence being committed.

Defence

It is a defence for the accused trespasser to show that:

- he or she did not know of the removal direction;

- the direction did not apply to him or her because he or she was not present on the land when the direction was issued; or
- his or her failure to leave or remove the vehicle or other property as soon as practicable or his or her re-entry with a vehicle was due to illness, mechanical breakdown or other immediate emergency.

The defendant can also apply for the proceedings to be adjourned for him or her to seek judicial review of the decision to issue a removal direction. The grounds of such an application are usually that the local authority has failed to take into account the defendant's circumstances as required by the guidance referred to above.

Removal orders

As well as being able to prosecute trespassers who fail to comply with a removal direction, the local authority can apply to the magistrates for a removal order under section 78 of CJPOA 1994. This effectively authorises the authority to take necessary steps to remove the trespassers from the land.

Commencement of proceedings

Proceedings are commenced by way of 'complaint'. Once the complaint is received, the magistrates' clerk issues the summons which will be served by the court and/or the local authority.

Service of the summons

A summons issued pursuant to section 78 of CJPOA 1994 may be directed either to the occupant of a particular vehicle on the land in question or to all occupants of vehicles on the land in question, without naming them. The summons can be served in the same way as the removal direction (CJPOA 1994, s. 79—see p. 169 above).

Making an order

Once the magistrates are satisfied that there are persons and vehicles in which they are residing present on land within the authority's area in contravention of a direction given under section 77 of CJPOA 1994, they may make an order requiring the removal of any vehicle or other property and any person residing in it. It is a matter for the local authority and not for the magistrates to decide whether it was reasonable to give a removal direction under section 77 in the first place (*Shropshire CC v Wynne* (1997)). The order may authorise the local authority to take such steps as are reasonably necessary to ensure that the order is complied with. In particular, the order may authorise the authority to:

- enter on the land specified in the order, and
- take, in relation to any vehicle or property to be removed in pursuance of the order, such steps for securing entry and making it suitable for removal as may be specified in the order.

Before entering any occupied land, the authority must give the owner and occupier of the land at least 24 hours' notice of its intention to do so unless, after reasonable inquiries, it cannot ascertain their names and addresses.

Any person who wilfully obstructs a person exercising powers under such an order commits a summary offence. The maximum fine is currently £1,000.

Challenge to a removal direction or removal order

If the local authority makes the decision to issue a removal direction without taking into consideration all the factors outlined above, the decision can be challenged by the trespassers bringing proceedings for judicial review. If the trespassers are successful, the removal direction is quashed. Additionally, any removal order made as a result of the removal direction will also fall (see the 'Case report' below). Equally, the only way to challenge a removal order (except on the basis that it is formally defective) is to attack the removal direction on which it is based by way of judicial review. It is therefore important that all the guidance and the other matters set out above are taken into consideration before a decision is made to issue a removal direction.

Case report

Two local authorities gave removal directions to people unlawfully camped on land in the locality and, as a result, the local magistrates made removal orders against all those who had not left and some who had arrived since the directions were given. The occupiers sought judicial review of the decision to issue removal directions. The High Court held that the guidance in paragraphs 10–13 of DoE Circular No 18/94 (see pp. 167–168 above) were considerations of common humanity and were therefore relevant considerations for the local authority in deciding whether to issue the directions. The authority therefore had to apply its mind to the circumstances of the people in occupation of the land and balance this against the needs of local residents. A removal direction therefore cannot apply to a person who arrives after it has been issued as the local authority would not have given any consideration to his or her individual circumstances. The authority should review its decision where there were relevant changes in the circumstances of the individuals concerned. *R v Wealden DC, ex p Wales; R v Same, ex p Stratford; R v Lincolnshire CC, ex p Atkinson* (1995)

Key points

- Local authorities can give removal directions to persons living in vehicles on open land which require them to leave.
- Before issuing a removal direction, the authority must have regard to considerations of common humanity; where the

trespassers are gypsies, the authority must have regard to all the matters in DoE Circular 18/94.

- It is an offence to fail to leave the land as soon as practicable after being served with a removal direction.
- The magistrates can then make a removal order entitling the authority to remove the occupiers and their vehicles.
- Occupiers can challenge a removal direction or removal order by judicial review.

18.

Summary Proceedings and Police Action

Summary proceedings on open land / Removal of trespassers by the police / Other offences

Summary proceedings on open land

Summary proceedings are discussed in detail in Chapter 10 above. They are quicker for open land than for residential premises as the notice of application has to be served on the occupiers only two clear days before the hearing.

A social landlord can apply for an order for possession of an area of land even where not all of it is occupied by trespassers. If it appears there is a likelihood of the trespassers merely moving to another part of the area in question, the court can make an order for the whole area. Similarly the highways authority can apply for an order of possession where only the highway verge is actually occupied; it is not necessary for the highway to be totally obstructed.

Unlike removal directions, it is not necessary for a local authority expressly to consider the matters referred to in DoE Circular 18/94 (see pp. 167–168 above) before deciding to institute summary possession proceedings.

Case report

Hillingdon LBC owned a caravan site and discovered that one of the sites was occupied without its permission by two brothers. Inquiries were made of the social services and health department and the council decided to issue summary possession proceedings. By the time they were issued, the brothers had moved and the site had been occupied by Mr McDonagh and his family. His solicitors wrote to the council saying that it was under a duty to carry out inquiries in relation to its statutory duties. The children were at a local school and there were health problems in the family which had been treated at the local hospital. Mr McDonagh sought judicial review of the council's decision to continue with possession proceedings.

The court held that the council was not obliged to observe the guidance in DoE Circular 18/94. The judge accepted that there was a duty on the council to act with 'common humanity', but held that the content of that duty depended on the circumstances. In this case, Mr McDonagh and his children were trespassers and there was no obligation on the authority to carry out detailed inquiries in relation to its statutory duties before deciding to evict them. *R v Hillingdon LBC, ex p McDonagh* (1998); see also *R v Brighton and Hove Council, ex p Marmont* (1998)

Execution of order for possession

Where summary proceedings are brought and an order made, the landlord has three months in which to issue the warrant. If it fails to apply for a warrant within that time it must ask the court for leave to issue it. In summary proceedings, which are intended to be quick, leave may not be granted unless there is good reason for any delay.

One common problem is that, even when one group of trespassers is successfully evicted, the land quickly becomes re-occupied. Clearly this can be avoided to a certain degree if the land is fenced off in some way after the first eviction, but in many cases this is neither desirable nor practicable. In such a case, where one warrant for possession has already been executed, a landlord can apply to the court for a warrant of restitution, which is effectively a second warrant of possession.

It is only available where there is a sufficient connection between the first and second periods of occupation. It is not necessary, however, for all those who are in occupation during the second period to have been on the land at the time the possession order was made. Where the two periods of occupation are entirely unconnected, it is necessary to apply for a further possession order. As those who habitually occupy open land tend to return to the same areas it is often the case that there is some sufficient connection.

Defences

The main defences to possession proceedings are discussed in Chapter 15 above. The defences most commonly raised in respect of open land are of adverse possession (which applies equally to all social landlords) or, where the local authority is seeking possession, that the decision to bring possession proceedings is unreasonable.

The county court does not have power to determine the question of whether the decision to bring possession proceedings is unreasonable. Therefore, the occupier must ask for the proceedings to be adjourned for him or her to make an application for judicial review. The judge should only adjourn the possession proceedings if there is a real chance of the occupier being granted leave to apply for judicial review. Where gypsies are involved, there may be some chance of leave being granted where there are no local authority gypsy sites in the area.

Removal of trespassers by the police

The police have powers under section 61 of CJPOA 1994 to remove people trespassing on open land where certain conditions are satisfied. The powers are also available where the people were not originally trespassers but have become trespassers because any permission they had to remain on the land has been withdrawn. Before these powers can be exercised the occupier must have taken reasonable steps to ask the trespassers to leave. For social landlords, this means that the relevant officer or employee must require the trespassers to vacate the land before any contact is made with the police. This could be done by delivering a notice to the trespassers informing them that they are not authorised to be on the land, that any permission they may have been given is now revoked and that they must vacate the land by a specified date.

The conditions for the police to take action are as follows. The senior police officer on the scene must reasonably believe that:

- there are two or more persons trespassing on the land;
- they are present there with the common purpose of residing there for any period; and
- reasonable steps have been taken by or on behalf of the occupier to ask them to leave.

He must also believe that:

- any of the trespassers has either caused damage to the land or property on the land or has used threatening, abusive or insulting words towards the occupier, a member of his or her family, his or her employee or agent; or
- the trespassers have between them six or more vehicles on the land.

For our purposes, the use of threatening, abusive or insulting words would be towards the social landlord's employees or agents. Any officer who experiences abuse should make a careful record of what was said, by whom and when.

When these conditions are satisfied, the senior police officer present may direct all or some of the trespassers to leave the land and to remove any vehicles or other property they have with them.

These powers do not apply to land which includes buildings which are not agricultural or ancient monuments, nor do they apply to most highways. They do, however, apply to common land. Where the common is one to which the public have access, the local authority is treated as the occupier.

Offences

A person who is trespassing on land when a direction is given by the police and who knows of the direction commits an offence if he or she:
- fails to leave the land as soon as reasonably practicable; or
- having left the land enters it again as a trespasser within three months beginning with the day on which the direction was given.

The offence is summary, and the maximum penalty is three months' imprisonment or a fine, currently of up to £2,500.

Defences

It is a defence for the accused to show that he or she:
- was not trespassing on the land; or
- had a reasonable excuse for failing to leave the land or re-entering the land as a trespasser.

A 'reasonable excuse' is not defined, but will be a question of fact in the circumstances of the case. An accused is also not guilty of an offence if he or she:
- was not in occupation of the land when the direction was made; or
- did not know of the direction.

Powers of seizure

Where a direction has been given under section 61 and a constable reasonably suspects that any person who was present on the land when the direction was given and without reasonable excuse has:
- failed to remove any vehicle on the land which appears to belong to him or her or be in his or her possession or under his or her control, or
- entered the land as a trespasser with a vehicle within three months of the day on which the direction was given,

the constable may seize and remove the vehicle (CJPOA 1994, s. 62). Where a social landlord is aware that a direction under section 61 has been made and the trespassers have failed to leave or have returned, the police should be informed immediately so that the trespassers' vehicles may be removed.

Other offences

The CJPOA 1994 creates several other trespass-related offences. These are not specifically related to occupation, however, and any detailed consideration of them is beyond the scope of this book. They are set out in outline below.

Sections 63–67 of CJPOA 1994 contain the provisions in relation to raves. The police have powers in certain circumstances to give directions ordering persons attending or preparing for a rave to leave the property. It is an offence to fail to leave the land as soon as practicable or to return within seven days. The police have powers of entry and seizure of equipment. Sound equipment can be forfeited by the court in certain circumstances.

The offence of aggravated trespass is created by section 68 of CJPOA 1994. This occurs where persons trespass on land intending to disrupt, obstruct or deter any lawful activity taking place on that or neighbouring land. This section was specifically aimed at hunt saboteurs.

Key points

- Summary proceedings in respect of open land are quick.
- There is no requirement for local authorities to consider the guidance laid down by Circular 18/94.
- The warrant for possession must be executed within three months; if the land is reoccupied, the landlord can apply for a warrant of restitution.
- Where the landlord has taken all reasonable steps to ask occupiers to leave, the police have power to remove them from the land.
- The police have power to seize any vehicles left on the land.

Glossary

Affidavit A formal statement written by a witness and made on oath to be used in court.

Allocation The process by which the court allocates a case to the small claims track, the fast track or the multi-track.

Applicant A person bringing an application.

Assignee A person to whom property has been assigned (or transferred).

Assignment The transfer of a property right from one person to another.

Assignor The person who assigns (or transfers) property to another.

Assured tenancy A tenancy that fulfils all the conditions set out in HA 1988. An assured tenancy can only be granted after 15 January 1989 by landlords who are housing associations or in the private sector.

Burden of proof The obligation on one party to prove any matter in issue in the proceedings.

Committal Proceedings brought by one party to enforce the terms of an order of the court, usually an injunction or an undertaking. The party in default can be fined or sent to prison.

Common law A phrase used to describe the law that comes from case-law rather than from statutes.

Covenant A term in a tenancy agreement in which one or other of the parties agrees to act in a certain way (e.g. to pay rent or to carry out repairs).

Directions An order by the court laying down the procedural steps and the timetable to be complied with in the preparation of an action for trial.

Disclosure The production by each party of all the documents in its possession which are relevant to the case.

Exclusive possession Exclusive possession of premises entitles the tenant to exclude all others, including the landlord, from the premises.

Fast track The normal procedural track for cases worth £5,000–15,000. A case which is allocated to the fast track will have a trial date to be within 30 weeks of allocation and should be dealt with in one day.

Forfeiture The process by which a landlord may terminate a lease if the tenant breaches any of the covenants.

Fixed-term tenancy A tenancy for a set period (e.g. for 12 months or 99 years). It comes to an end automatically at the end of the period.

Head landlord Where a tenant sublets to a subtenant, the tenant's immediate landlord is known as the head landlord.

Injunction An order of the court that someone should do certain acts or refrain from doing certain acts.

Informal admission A statement made by a party which is contrary to that party's case.

Interlocutory Used to describe applications in the course of proceedings. It is most commonly used to describe injunctions to mean an interim injunction made pending the hearing of the final action.

Licence An agreement other than a tenancy by which the owner of land permits another person to be present or do something on the land.

Multi-track The normal procedural track for cases worth over £15,000 and those where the trial is likely to take more than one day.

Negligence Failing to take reasonable care to ensure that a person is safe from injury or loss. The duty to take such care is not imposed in all circumstances.

Notice seeking possession A notice served on a secure or assured tenant by the landlord before possession proceedings can be brought, specifying the grounds on which proceedings are being brought.

Notice to quit A formal notice from a landlord to a tenant without security of tenure requiring the tenant to leave the premises.

Nuisance The interference with the enjoyment of a tenant or owner of his or her land.

Particulars of claim A formal statement of the claimant's case.

Periodic tenancy A tenancy which is not for a fixed term but is set in terms of a regular period, usually the period in relation to which rent is paid. A periodic tenancy automatically renews itself unless the landlord or tenant gives notice to quit.

Return date The date set by the court for the hearing of a summons for possession.

Secure licence A licence which fulfils the conditions set out in HA 1985, granted by local authorities or, before 15 January 1989, housing associations. The licence must be one which confers exclusive possession on the occupier. A secure licence has the same statutory protection as a secure tenancy.

Secure tenancy A tenancy which fulfils the conditions set out in HA 1985, granted by local authorities or, before 15 January 1989, housing associations.

Security of tenure A tenant who is either secure or assured has security of tenure.

Small-claims track The normal procedural track for cases worth less than £5,000.

Statement of case The formal statements made by each party of their case. They include the particulars of claim and the defence.

Subletting (or subtenancy) Where someone who is themselves a tenant grants a tenancy of the premises to another, this is known as a subletting.

Subtenant The tenant under a subtenancy.

Tenancy An agreement giving exclusive possession of property for a period (either fixed term or periodic) and usually for a rent.

Index

Also available in Arden's Housing Library

Allocating Social Housing

Law and practice in the management of social housing
Hal Pawson, David Mullins & Siobhan McGrath

This handbook is a guide to the law and practice governing lettings for both new applicants and existing tenants of local authorities and registered social landlords. As well as explaining the relevant legislation, regulatory guidance, and decided cases, the authors also draw on research evidence to describe social landlords' policies and best practice in the management of allocations.

Guidance is given on all key issues:

- Maintenance of housing registers and information to housing applicants.
- Transfer eligibility, contractual succession and landlord's interest moves.
- Assessing housing needs, offers and refusals, appeals procedures.
- Groups qualifying for 'reasonable preference'.
- Applying equal opportunities in allocations.
- Nominations and assistance to local authorities.
- Performance indicators.
- How to deal with fraudulent applications.

Chapter contents
The changing context • Discrimination in allocations • Access to social housing • Mobility within social housing • Social housing allocation schemes: systems and objectives • Allocation of local authority housing • Allocation of housing by registered social landlords • Monitoring of allocations.

About the authors
Hal Pawson is a Research Fellow at the School of Housing and Planning, Heriot-Watt University, Edinburgh. David Mullins is a Senior Lecturer at the Centre for Urban and Regional Studies, University of Birmingham. Siobhan McGrath is lawyer Vice-President of the London Rent Assessment Panel and a barrister of Arden Chambers.

ISBN: 1-898001-53-7
Published Spring 2000
Available directly from Plymbridge Distributors Ltd. Tel 01752 202301 or Fax 01752 202333

Also available in Arden's Housing Library

Houses in Multiple Occupation

Law and practice in the management of social housing

Andrew Dymond, Barrister

The law can ensure that houses in multiple occupation provide safe, comfortable housing at a reasonable price. This book helps those working for this aim with clear and concise guidance on the general and special powers available to local authorities including:

- The establishment of registration schemes.
- Powers to serve and enforce notices on owners or managers to remedy unsafe conditions, overcrowding, poor repair or badly management.
- Standards that should be maintained and assistance available.
- Duties in relation to common problems associated with HMOs.
- Responsibilities for rehousing and compensation.

Chapter contents

Definitions • Registration Schemes • Conditions, Facilities and Overcrowding • Enforcement • Paying for Repairs and Improvements • Day-to-day Management and Occupiers' Rights • Rehousing Tenants

About the Author

Andrew Dymond is a barrister and member of Arden Chambers. He is also the author of *Security of Tenure* and *Presenting Possession Proceedings*, also published in Arden's Housing Library.

ISBN: 1-898001-16-2
Published Spring 2000
Available directly from Plymbridge Distributors Ltd. Tel. 01752 202301 or Fax 01752 202333

Also available in Arden's Housing Library

Security of Tenure

Law and practice in the management of social housing
Second edition
Andrew Dymond, Barrister

This completely revised and up-to-date edition explains in accessible language the legal framework within which a housing manager is working on any given case, demonstrating the options available in the management of a tenancy. An appendix includes all required model letters and forms for use in casework. Guidance in key areas is given including:

- Procedures for creating different kinds of tenancy.
- Identifying which Act applies to the tenancy.
- What rights exist to remain in the property.
- The circumstances in which security of tenure may be lost.
- The powers landlords have to terminate the tenancy.
- Procedures for termination by the landlord and re-gaining possession.

Chapter contents
Status of the Occupier • Tenant or Licensee? • Secure and Assured Tenancies • Conditions for Security of Tenure • Seeking Possession • Grounds for Possession Against Secure Tenants • Grounds for Possession Against Assured Tenants • Suitable Alternative Accommodation • Reasonableness • Other Occupiers • Possession Orders • Termination by the Tenant

About the Author
Andrew Dymond is a barrister and member of Arden Chambers. He is also the author of *Presenting Possession Proceedings*, also published in Arden's Housing Library.

ISBN: 1-898001-63-4
Published Spring 2000
Available directly from Plymbridge Distributors Ltd. Tel. 01752 202301 or Fax 01752 202333

Also available in Arden's Housing Library

Discrimination and Social Housing

Law and practice in the management of social housing
Alyson Kilpatrick, Barrister

This book is a tool for making real the objectives of the anti-discrimination legislation on sex, race and disability. Clearly spelling out the practical implications of the codes of guidance and the law—including the new Human Rights Act—the book is as helpful in establishing where positive action is legitimate as it is in pointing out indirectly discriminatory practices. Access to accommodation, housing management issues, as well as selection and employment of staff are all covered; guidance by the author is provided on all key problems including:

- How to assess allegations and legal responsibility for unfair treatment on grounds of race, sex or disability.
- Responsibility to tackle harassment.
- Responsibility to have fair treatment in relation to recruitment, selection, employment and dismissal.

Chapter contents
Legal Framework • Enforcement of the Legislation • Discrimination on Grounds of Race or Sex • Disability • Sexual Orientation • General Public Duties • Monitoring • Housing Services • Housing Allocation and Homeless • Dealing with Harassment • Discrimination in Employment.

About the Author
Alyson Kilpatrick is a barrister and member of Arden Chambers. She is the author of *Repairs and Maintenance*, also published in Arden's Housing Library.

ISBN: 1-898001-34-0
Published Spring 2000
Available directly from Plymbridge Distributors Ltd. Tel 01752-202301 or Fax 01752 202333

Also available in Arden's Housing Library

RSL Finance and Rents

Law and practice in the management of social housing
William Okoya, Barrister

The financial environment in which registered social landlords (RSL) operate is complex: on the one hand heavily regulated and proceduralised, and on the other, commercial and competitive. This new book in Arden's Housing Library explains the legal framework and structures consistent with the need to become more commercial whilst providing decent affordable homes for people in need. Accessible guidance is given on all key issues including:

- What systems and resources must be in place to comply with regulatory requirements.
- How to make applications and bids for special grants and funding.
- How to deal with the consequences of various types of private finance.
- What policies and procedures should be used for rent setting and collection.
- How to deal with liabilities for corporation tax, capital gains tax, non-domestic rates, stamp duty and VAT.

Chapter contents
Registered Social Landlords • Regulatory Framework • Public Subsidy and Finance of RSLs • Private Finance and Investment in RSLs • Rent and Housing Benefit • Taxation • Mergers and acquisitions, group structures, and partnerships and consortia.

About the Author
William Okoya is a barrister and member of Arden Chambers.

ISBN: 1-898001-52-9
Published Spring 2000
Available directly from Plymbridge Distributors Ltd. Tel 01752 202301 or Fax 01752 202333

Also available in Arden's Housing Library

Children and Housing

Law and practice in the management of social housing
Josephine Henderson, Barrister

All children need to be adequately housed, but there is a variety of ways in which this may be achieved, and problems to which this may give rise. Thus some children need to be housed with their parents, and to house the children may require rehousing the whole family. On the other hand, some children may not have any support from their family, may have left home, or may be in the care of the local authority. In this case, very different considerations may arise in seeking to provide adequate housing. What can and should authorities and other landlords provide for the individual child? What are the legal consequences of providing housing for children. Once housed it may be that children are in fact a problem (e.g. through anti-social behaviour), or that although housing is provided it is not adequate for the child (e.g. because the child is disabled, or because the condition of the house makes the child ill). This book addresses these practical problems and many others in providing comprehensive coverage of housing issues as they affect children.

Chapter contents
Assessments under the Housing Act 1996, Part VII • Accommodation provision under the Housing Act 1996, Part VII • Key duties to provide accommodation and other services under the Children Act 1989 • Assessments under the Children Act • Accommodation provision under the Children Act • Responsibility for children in care and young people who have left care • Benefits and grants available to young people, families and housing providers • Duties to co-operate imposed on housing and social services authorities • Methods of resolving disputes

About the Author
Josephine Henderson is a barrister and member of Arden Chambers. She is the author of *Rights to Buy and Acquire*, also published in Arden's Housing Library.

ISBN: 1-898001-20-0
Published Spring 2000
Available directly from Plymbridge Distributors Ltd. Tel 01752-202301 or Fax 01752-202333

Also available in Arden's Housing Library

Tied Accommodation

Law and practice in the management of social housing
Dominic Preston, Barrister

This book explains the rights, responsibilities and housing management issues in dealing with staff living in accommodation as part of their employment ñ such as caretakers and teachers in schools, wardens in sheltered accommodation, social workers, park-keepers and others. Guidance is given on all key problem areas including:

- How to distinguish a tenancy from a licence.
- How to distinguish a service tenancy from service occupancies under the Housing Act 1985 and the Housing Act 1988.
- How introductory tenancies are created and terminated. Special grounds for possession of a secure tenancy.
- How to terminate assured and assured shorthold tenancies.
- How to terminate fixed term and periodic tenancies.
- How to terminate non-secure licences. Possession and dismissal.
- How to deal with right to buy or acquire; disrepair; rent increases; variation of rent and dismissal.

Chapter contents
Tenancy or Licence? • Categories of Tied Occupier. • Secure Tenants and Licensees. • Assured Tenants. • Termination of Non-secure Tenancies. • Termination of Non-secure Licences. • Housing Management Issues.

About the Author
Dominic Preston is a barrister and member of Arden Chambers.

ISBN: 1-898001-49-9
Published Spring 2000
Available directly from Plymbridge Distributors Ltd. Tel 01752 202301 or Fax 01752 202333

Also available in Arden's Housing Library

A Guide to the Planning Process

Law and practice in the management of social housing

Iain Colville, Barrister

This book provides practical legal guidance on the steps that must be taken from the first day it has been decided to carry out any housing development to the day on which the decision of the authority is finally resolved. Issues on which guidance is given include:

- How an authority should prepare a development plan and how RSLs can be involved.
- What types of work require planning permission?
- How to proceed with the application, steps to take before and after it is made.
- What an authority can and cannot take into account when determining the application.
- How appeals are made procedure and the steps to be followed by parties involved.
- Powers and procedures to deal with development carried out without consent.
- Powers to protect the environment.

Chapter contents

The Development Plan • The Meaning of 'Development' • The Planning Application • The Determination • Inquiries and Appeals • Enforcement Powers • Special Controls

About the Author

Iain Colville is a practising barrister specialising in local planning and is a member of Arden Chambers.

ISBN: 1-898001-51-0
Published Spring 2000
Available directly from Plymbridge Distributors Ltd. Tel 01752 202301 or Fax 01752 202333

Also available in Arden's Housing Library

Tenants' Rights

Law and practice in the management of social housing
Caroline Hunter, Barrister

'Caroline Hunter has written very clearly and concisely and made extremely good use of case law.' *The Adviser*

Secure tenants of councils and housing associations have more control over their homes than ever before—and keeping abreast of these rights is essential for housing professionals. This guide covers rights to succession, taking in lodgers, exchanging homes and subletting. Tenants' collective rights to information, to manage, to change their landlord are also included.

Chapter contents
Historical Background • Succession • Assignment, Lodgers and Subletting • Changing the Terms of the Tenancy • Information and Consultation • The Right to Manage • Estate Redevelopment

About the Author
Caroline Hunter lectures at the University of Nottingham and is a barrister at Arden Chambers. She specialises in housing, landlord and tenant, local government powers, finance and proceedings, competitive tendering and environmental health. She is the author (with Andy Selman) of *CCT of Housing Management* and (with Kerry Bretherton) of *Anti-social Behaviour* (Arden's Housing Library), and also many other specialist practitioner works including Arden & Hunter's *Local Government Finance Law and Practice*.

ISBN 1-898001-13-8
Published 1995
Available directly from Plymbridge Distributors Ltd. Tel 01752 202301 or Fax 01752 202333

Also available in Arden's Housing Library

Anti-social Behaviour

Law and practice in the management of social housing
Caroline Hunter, Barrister and Kerry Bretherton, Barrister

Anti-social behaviour is a growing problem that is taxing housing managers and others. This new book looks at remedies available for landlords against tenants and other perpetrators, as well as setting out the landlord's liability to third parties. Special treatment is given to specific problems such as violence, drug dealing, pets, noise, and behaviour motivated by prejudice. Guidance is given on the practical problems involved in enforcement and bringing cases to court.

Chapter contents
Providing a Comprehensive Approach • Liability of the Landlord for Anti-social Behaviour • Introductory Tenancies • Nuisance Behaviour by Tenants • Nuisance Behaviour by Particular Groups • Specific Problems • Behaviour Motivated by Prejudice • In Court

About the Authors
Caroline Hunter is a barrister at Arden Chambers and lectures at the University of Nottingham. She specialises in housing, landlord and tenant, local government powers, finance and proceedings, competitive tendering and environmental health. She is the author of *Tenants' Rights* and, with Andy Selman, *CCT of Housing Management* (Arden's Housing Library) and many other specialist practitioner works including Arden & Hunter's *Local Government Finance Law and Practice*.

Kerry Bretherton is a barrister at Arden Chambers and specialises in housing, landlord and tenant, and environmental health.

ISBN 1-898001-37-5
Published 1998
Available directly from Plymbridge Distributors Ltd. Tel 01752 202301 or Fax 01752 202333

Also available in Arden's Housing Library

Presenting Possession Proceedings

Law and practice in the management of social housing
Andrew Dymond, Barrister

'Housing managers and officers involved in regaining possession should find this book invaluable.' *ADC Review*

With pressure to maximise rent and minimise management costs, more and more housing managers are finding themselves handling possession proceedings. This book provides expert guidance through that process: how to gather evidence and begin the proceedings; how to use pre-trial and trial court procedures and what orders to apply for. Checklists and model forms are included to make sure proceedings do not run into the sand because of error or omission.

Chapter contents
Commencing Possession Proceedings • What Needs to be Proved? • The Return Date • Pre-Trial Procedure • Evidence • The Trial • Rent Arrears Cases • Other Types of Possession Action • Possession Orders • Further Action • Court Forms

About the Author
Andrew Dymond is a barrister at Arden Chambers and specialises in housing, landlord and tenant, environmental health and social security. He is author of *Security of Tenure* and *Houses in Multiple Occupation* (Arden's Housing Library) and editor, *Housing Encyclopaedia*, *Housing Law Reports* and *Journal of Housing Law.*

ISBN 1-898001-15-4
Published 1996
Available directly from Plymbridge Distributors Ltd. Tel 01752 202301 or Fax 01752 202333